TO THE PACIFIC WITH
LEWIS AND CLARK

CHINOOK

BLACKFOOT

MINNETAREE (ATSINA)

CHINOOK
Cape Disappointment
Fort Clatsop
CLATSOP

LEWIS AND CLARK PASS

◄ LEWIS 1806 ►

LEWIS 1806 ►

TILLAMOOK

Columbia

Snake River

1805 ◄

Great Falls

LEWIS AND CLARK

Traveler's Rest

The Dalles ✕

LEWIS AND CLARK 1806 ◄

GATES OF THE MOUNTAINS

NEZ PERCE

Clearwater R.

LOLO TRAIL

Three Forks ✕

CLARK 1806 ►

Salmon R.

Lemhi R.

BOZEMAN PASS

Yellowstone River

Bighorn River

OREGON COUNTRY

Willamette River

CASCADE MOUNTAINS

Bitterroot R.

Jefferson R.

Madison R.

Gallatin R.

SHOSHONI

ROCKY MOUNTAINS

Snake River

COAST RANGES

SIERRA NEVADA

SPANISH POSSESSIONS

CONTINENTAL DIVIDE

PACIFIC OCEAN

0   50   100   150
SCALE OF MILES

TO THE PACIFIC WITH

LEWIS AND CLARK

BY THE EDITORS OF AMERICAN HERITAGE, *The Magazine of History*

AUTHOR: RALPH K. ANDRIST

CONSULTANT: EDWIN R. BINGHAM, *Professor of History, University of Oregon*

PUBLISHED BY AMERICAN HERITAGE PUBLISHING CO., INC.

BOOK TRADE AND INSTITUTIONAL DISTRIBUTION BY HARPER & ROW

FIRST EDITION FOURTH PRINTING

© 1967 by American Heritage Publishing Co., Inc., 551 Fifth Avenue, New York, New York 10017. All rights reserved under Berne and Pan-American Copyright Conventions. Library of Congress Catalog Card Number: 67-24547. Trademark AMERICAN HERITAGE JUNIOR LIBRARY registered United States Patent Office.

A century after Lewis and Clark reached the Columbia estuary in 1805, Charles M. Russell painted their meeting with a Chinook Indian canoe party. In this detail Lewis (right) stands by Sacagawea, who addresses the Chinooks in signs.

FOREWORD

The object of your mission is to explore the Missouri river & such principal stream of it, as, by it's course and communication with the waters of the Pacific ocean . . . may offer the most direct & practicable water communication across this continent for the purposes of commerce.

With these words President Thomas Jefferson, in June, 1803, outlined the chief purpose of one of the most important expeditions in American history: the first charting of the vast territory added to the United States by the Louisiana Purchase. Neither of its captains was a trained explorer, or scientist, or doctor, or diplomat, although Meriwether Lewis and William Clark filled all these roles in the course of their epic journey. They were observant, resourceful, experienced Army officers, accustomed to frontier command, who equipped and disciplined their little party so well that it covered the 7,689 miles to the Pacific Ocean and back with the loss of only one life and with only one actively hostile encounter with Indians.

This account of the Lewis and Clark expedition contains many extracts from the captains' own journals, which recount each day's events in fascinating detail—and ingenious spelling. To re-create their journey in visual terms, modern photographs have been combined with Clark's original maps and drawings, contemporary portraits and engravings, and paintings by artists who depicted the West before it was engulfed by the tide of emigration that followed so swiftly in the expedition's wake.

According to Lewis' final accounting, the total cost of the expedition was $38,722.25—surely a bargain price for an enterprise that opened up the Louisiana Territory to trappers, traders, and emigrants, affirmed the United States' claim to the Oregon country, and inspired each succeeding generation of Americans with an unparalleled story of courage, devotion, and success.

THE EDITORS

RIGHT: *A silver medal given by Lewis and Clark to a Nez Percé chief was found in 1899.*
AMERICAN MUSEUM OF NATURAL HISTORY, NEW YORK

COVER: *In the misty hills above Idaho's sparkling Lochsa River the men nearly perished.*
RAY ATKESON

FRONT ENDSHEET: *The expedition's routes to the Pacific and back are shown on a map.*

TITLE PAGE: *Where Yellowstone and Missouri meet, the divided expedition was reunited.*
MAXIMILIAN, *Travels in the Interior* . . . , 1834: YALE UNIVERSITY LIBRARY

BACK ENDSHEET: *After a twentieth-century storm, Pacific surf foams on an Oregon beach.*
RAY ATKESON

BACK COVER: *This sketch of a "cock of the plains" comes from one of Clark's journals.*
MISSOURI HISTORICAL SOCIETY

CONTENTS

1

THOMAS JEFFERSON'S DREAM

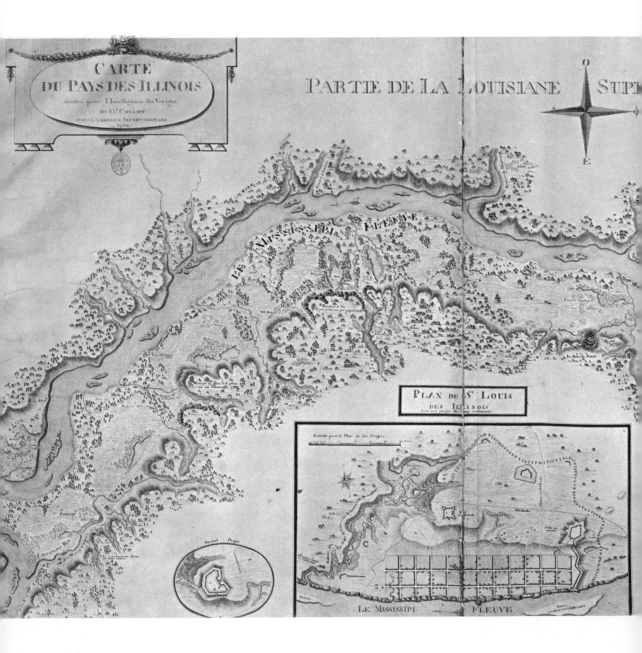

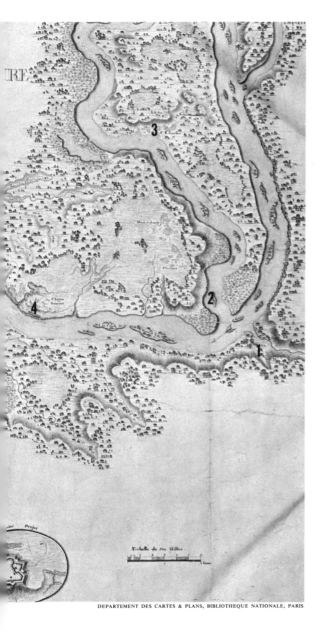

It was the evening of May 14, 1804. After a rainy, gusty day, night was beginning to close in on the row of neatly pitched tents, the sputtering campfire, and the three heavily laden boats moored by the bank of the island in the middle of the Missouri River. The tall, redheaded officer probably watched the muddy Missouri water, full of snags and eddies, swirling past the little encampment for a while before he turned to enter his tent. There he lit a lantern, carefully mixed up a fresh supply of powdered ink and water in his inkhorn, and set to work writing up his notes for the day. From outside came the sound of eager conversation in French and English as his forty-two men, in high spirits despite the rain, discussed the adventure on which they were setting forth and told tall tales of gigantic savages, "particularly hostile to white men," and of other marvels

A 1796 French map shows the area around St. Louis (inset), which was to become Lewis and Clark's 1804 departure point. Leaving winter quarters (1), Clark camped on a Missouri island (2) en route to St. Charles (3). Lewis rode from St. Louis (4) to join him.

11

awaiting them in the unexplored country ahead.

But when Captain William Clark began to write, he had little to say. In a matter-of-fact first paragraph he told that it had rained that morning and that he planned to join Captain Meriwether Lewis, coleader of the expedition, at the village of St. Charles some twenty-one miles up the Missouri from St. Louis. Then, in an equally brief second paragraph, he told about the departure of the expedition from the tiny camp opposite the mouth of the Missouri where they had spent the months of preparation:

I Set out at 4 oClock P.M., in the presence of many of the neighbouring inhabitents, and proceeded on under a jentle brease up the Missouri to the upper Point of the 1st Island 4 Miles and camped on the Island which is Situated Close on the right (or Starboard) Side, and opposit the mouth of a Small Creek called Cold water, a heavy rain this after-noon

And that was all Captain Clark had to say about the first day of one of the greatest adventures in American history. He and his companions were embarking on a four-thousand-mile journey to the Pacific Ocean and back. He and Captain Lewis would be opening a trail where white men had never gone before. But Clark was seldom an emotional man, and at that moment he was probably more conscious of the responsibilities that weighed upon him than of the excitements ahead. His years of experience as an army commander had taught him the value

of traveling only a small distance from base at the outset of an expedition, so that anything left behind could be quickly fetched and any loading problems dealt with speedily. But although he had just spent five months in camp, toughening his men physically and teaching both raw recruits and regular soldiers a very rigorous discipline, there were still rough edges to be smoothed off before they would be ready to meet the tremendous challenges of the trip. Chosen as they had been for toughness and initiative, the men found military routine irksome, and whiskey drinking had been the only diversion of their drab winter.

Remembering this two days later, as the villagers of St. Charles welcomed them by arranging to hold a ball in their honor, Clark issued an order: "Note the Commanding officer is full assured that every man of his Detachment will have a true respect for their own Dignity and not make it necessary for him to leave St. Charles for a more retired situation."

His hopes were dashed—St. Charles was their last major stop in civilized territory, and the temptations of its whiskey and pretty girls were too great. Three of Clark's men went absent without leave to enjoy themselves, and one not only behaved "in an unbecomeing manner" at the ball but was disrespectful to his officers on returning. Clark ordered a court-martial before four enlisted men and Sergeant John Ordway. They pronounced a sentence of twenty-five

As pictured on an 1817 bank note, St. Louis is little bigger than the river town of 180 houses familiar to Lewis and Clark in 1804.

lashes each, with a recommendation for mercy, for two of the men absent without leave and fifty stripes for John Collins, who had also been drunk and disrespectful. Clark honored the plea for mercy and substituted a stiff warning for the lashes. But he made an example of Collins, who had to receive the full fifty lashes from his comrades' ramrods and switches on his "naked back." Insubordination could not be permitted in a military expedition with so much at stake. During the long trip ahead there would come times when the lives of the entire party would depend on each man doing exactly as he was ordered.

On Sunday, May 20, after three days of reloading the boats, taking on extra stores, and dancing in the evenings, Clark sent his men to the last church service they would attend for nearly two and a half years. That day, in the midst of a thunderstorm, Captain Meriwether Lewis rode into St. Charles. He had been arranging several last-minute details in St. Louis.

One of these was organizing a visit to Washington by a group of influential Indian chiefs. Another was saying farewell to some of the St. Louis belles, for Captain Lewis, a tall, fair-haired man who wore his uniform with an air, hid a romantic heart beneath his rather reserved exterior. A small troop of close friends had come along to say a final good-by. The next afternoon, May 21, the now-complete expedition departed at half-past three—another late start. As Lewis' friends gave three hearty cheers from the bank, the boats hoisted sail and set off upstream.

Four days and fifty miles later, the voyagers reached the tiny French village of La Charrette. They camped overnight at a nearby creek, where friendly villagers brought them milk and eggs. Another explorer, Daniel Boone, then an old man, was living near La Charrette, but if any member of the expedition knew it, he did not mention it in his journal.

The party was traveling in three boats. The largest was a keelboat, a type familiar on western rivers. It was fifty-five feet long, had a mast and a square sail for use when there was a favorable wind, and twenty oars for the far more frequent times when there was none. There was a ten-foot-deep deck forward and a small cabin aft.

OVERLEAF: *After their return from the Pacific the captains were painted by Charles Willson Peale, who added these portraits to his famous museum of American history and science in Independence Hall, Philadelphia.*

William Clark

Meriwether Lewis

Along each side were lockers for stores. Their lids, when raised, would form a protective wall if the boat were attacked. At each end, mounted on a swivel, was a small cannon that could be loaded with grapeshot to repel boarders. The two other craft were pirogues, sturdy boats shaped rather like flatirons. Like the keelboat, they could be sailed or rowed. The larger, painted red, had seven oars; the other, which was white, had six.

The party now numbered forty-five. Sixteen men—seven American soldiers and nine French watermen, expert at handling boats—would help the expedition only as far as the villages of the Mandan Indians, in what is now North Dakota, and would return the following spring. Two skilled watermen, Pierre Cruzatte and François Labiche, would act as permanent boatmen to the party. Fourteen regular soldiers and nine Kentucky volunteers had signed on for the entire trip. Nearly all were under thirty, and one, George Shannon, was only seventeen.

Each was healthy, hardy, single, and prepared to risk his life on a journey into uncharted territory for five dollars a month. The three sergeants got eight dollars each. An unpaid member of the crew was Clark's Negro slave, York, whom he always referred to as "my servant."

Apart from the two captains, the most valuable member of the party was the expedition's interpreter, George Drouilliard, who was also its chief hunter. Half French, half Indian, Drouilliard was an expert at sign language—the only means of communicating with unfamiliar Indian tribes—a skilled woodsman, and a crack shot. He earned twenty-five dollars a month and was worth every cent. The captains had trouble in spelling his name, so they wrote it down as it sounded to them. Drouilliard became Drewyer in their journals—and he will become Drewyer here.

Also aboard was Lewis' big Newfoundland dog, Scannon, who was to prove most valuable to the expedition.

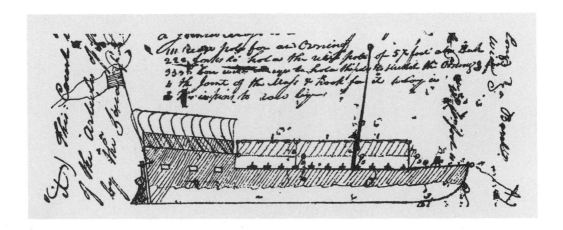

The first weeks went by without serious mishaps. Soon it was midsummer, a time of violent thunderstorms that came without warning, bringing lightning, torrents of rain, sudden gales, and sometimes hail. The swift-flowing Missouri was always dangerous, good weather or bad. Its banks were constantly caving in at one place while the currents built sand bars at another. Its countless bends were studded with snags—dead trees embedded in the mud—often with sharp stubs of branches just below the surface, ready to tear the bottom out of a boat. Although the men sweated in turn at oars, poles, and towlines, they were lucky if they covered fifteen miles in a day.

Hard as they worked their men, captains Lewis and Clark were equally active. In addition to navigation and the military command of the expedition, they had scores of observations to make about the country through which they passed. They made careful notes about the animals, plants, and minerals along the way. Every river and brook was described, and every hill, rock formation, or other feature worthy of mention was recorded. Each night Clark filled in more details on a map of their route, which was intended, like their voluminous notes, for the expedition's absent patron. For, as they fought their way upstream against the current, each mile took them farther from the visionary who had brought the group into being—the extraordinary man who was now the third President of the United States.

Thomas Jefferson himself had not been farther west then perhaps fifty miles beyond his home in Virginia, but for years his thoughts had reached out toward the Pacific Ocean. This was partly from curiosity, for Jefferson had a scientist's mind and was always eager to know about the plants and animals, the mountains and rivers, and especially the Indian tribes in the unknown country beyond the frontier. But his chief interest sprang from his conviction that the United States was

During the five months he spent training the expedition's volunteers and loading supplies, Clark scribbled notes about the trip ahead on every available sheet of paper. His sketch of the fifty-five-foot keelboat from the side (left) shows the raised cabin for himself and Lewis in the stern and the ridgepoles for the "Orning" amidships that would shield the rowers from the sun. The deck plan at right gives the arrangement of oars and benches for the twenty men who rowed the heavily laden keelboat up the Missouri.

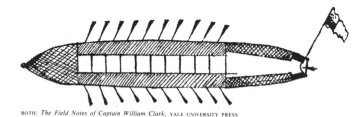

BOTH: *The Field Notes of Captain William Clark*, YALE UNIVERSITY PRESS

destined to expand westward. This made it vital that everything possible should be learned about the western lands. It had long been Jefferson's dream that Americans should traverse the Rocky Mountains and find the fabled Great River of the West that would lead them to the Pacific.

Nearly twenty years earlier, Jefferson had talked about such a journey with General George Rogers Clark, the Revolutionary hero and Captain William Clark's elder brother. General Clark had agreed that it was an excellent project but declined to lead it. Keep the expedition small, he advised Jefferson, no more than three or four men.

Not until 1787 did Jefferson have a chance to put his schemes into action —and then his plan was a harebrained one. While serving in Paris as United States Minister to France, he met John Ledyard, an American adventurer who had visited the Pacific Northwest with Captain Cook nine years earlier. Between them, the two men decided that Ledyard should cross Russia and Siberia to the Pacific Ocean, beg a ride on a Russian ship to the northwest coast of America, from which he would walk, completely alone, across the Rockies to the Missouri River and finally to civilization.

It was a wild scheme. Western America was unknown; the Columbia River had not yet been discovered; and the Empress Catherine of Russia forbade Ledyard to cross her lands. Yet in 1788 this unusual man managed

The French sculptor Jean Antoine Houdon modeled this bust of Thomas Jefferson in 1789 when the future President, aged forty-six, was United States Minister to France.

to evade the empress' orders and travel some 2,500 miles into Siberia before Catherine's displeasure caught up with him. Guards hustled Ledyard back across the country and dumped him over the border into Poland.

Four years later, in 1792, Jefferson was Secretary of State and back in the United States. He had a new plan, one not much more sensible than the last. He proposed to send André Michaux, a French botanist, up the Missouri and through the unknown country to the Pacific with a single companion. Meriwether Lewis, then eighteen years old, begged to go along with Michaux on the journey but was refused by Jefferson because he was too young. However, the project came to nothing when it was discovered that Michaux was a secret agent of the French government, whose real purpose was to stir up trouble between the newly formed American republic and the long-established Spanish colonies in the south and the west of the continent.

In 1801 Thomas Jefferson became President of the United States. At last he was in a unique position to organize his long-dreamed-of expedition to the Pacific. It would not only bring back information fascinating to Jefferson the scientist. By opening a new trade route across the continent, Americans could challenge Britain's domination of the Pacific Northwest and its fabulous harvest of furs—an attractive prospect to a President patriotically concerned with the future of his young republic.

Jefferson's election had been close and bitterly contested, and as he looked about for a personal secretary, he was more interested in finding a trustworthy aide-de-camp with whom he could talk over his problems than in employing someone to answer his letters. Even more than a confidant, the President needed a potential leader for his expedition, and his thoughts at once turned to the young man who, nine years before, had asked to go west with André Michaux—Meriwether Lewis.

Jefferson knew young Lewis well, for their two families lived not far apart in Albemarle County, Virginia. Meriwether's father had died during the Revolution, a great-uncle had married one of George Washington's sisters, and there were other prominent men in the family. Meriwether, the eldest son of a twice-widowed mother, had received an adequate but undistinguished education. The President's chief interest at the moment was that he had had six years' Army service on the frontier, gaining experience that would be valuable if he were later to travel into the Far West.

Jefferson sent off a letter to Lewis offering him the position of personal secretary to the President. The twenty-six-year-old captain, who was paymaster for the 1st United States Infantry Regiment, was just then making a swing through the Ohio country to pay the soldiers garrisoning the lonely frontier forts. He found the President's letter waiting when he got back to civilization at Pittsburgh in March, 1801, and instantly replied, accepting the office and thanking Jefferson for "this mark of your confidence and esteem."

As soon as he had handed over his neatly kept accounts, Lewis set out for Washington. The road was rough, and spring rains flooded the mountain trails, but the young captain was never happier than when "rambling" in wild country. With his muddy pack horses, he rode into Washington on April 1. The President had just left for Monticello, his home in Virginia, so Lewis followed him there. From that time on, whether at Monticello or at the newly erected White House, Meriwether Lewis lived as Jefferson had promised, "as . . . one of my family."

20

A GENTLEMAN OF GENIUS

"He who receives an idea from me, receives instruction himself without lessening mine," wrote Thomas Jefferson, one of the most brilliant men America has ever known. Philoso pher, lawyer, scientist, architect, classical scholar, violinist, plantation owner, inventor —Jefferson's extraordinary mind knew no barriers. Meriwether Lewis, who lived and worked for two years as his constant and intimate companion, received a kind of instruc- tion that was worth a lifetime of academic experience. Although Jefferson was twice elected President of the United States, he was always happiest at Monticello, the Virginia country house he designed and embellished with countless inventions. Below, a water color made in 1804 shows the President's home, still unfinished, in the year that Lewis went up the Missouri. Jefferson's ingenious clock still adorns the gracious entrance hall (left), flanked by elk and moose antlers presented to him by Lewis and Clark. Operated by a system of cannon-ball weights, the clock tells not only the time but also the days of the week as the weights descend against the wall. At lower left is one reason why Jefferson little needed a secretary: he copied his letters as he wrote them by using this polygraph, made to his own design, which operated two pens simultaneously. Preparing for Lewis' trip, the President even worked out a special cipher for their secret correspondence.

It is a pity the young secretary did not keep a diary of the things he discussed with the President when they were alone. But there is no doubt that their conversations turned early and often to the subject of the Pacific expedition. In 1802 Lewis was already beginning to organize such an expedition, and in 1803 he began actively collecting equipment and estimating expenses. In February, 1803, Jefferson wrote confidentially to a friend:

Capt. Lewis is brave, prudent, habituated to the woods, & familiar with Indian manners & character. He is not regularly educated, but he possesses a great mass of accurate observation on all the subjects of nature which present themselves here, & will therefore readily select those only in his new route which shall be new. He has qualified himself for those observations of longitude & latitude necessary to fix the points of the line he will go over.

The note had to be confidential because the planned expedition would be in foreign territory once it crossed the Mississippi, and Jefferson did not want the Spaniards or the French to think of it as anything more than a peaceful scientific exploration.

The French had originally colonized the Louisiana country after the great explorer Robert Cavelier, Sieur de La Salle, followed the Mississippi to its mouth in 1682. Claiming the vast valley drained by the river and its branches, he named the whole area Louisiana for his monarch, Louis XIV. Thoroughly French towns and settlements grew up: New Orleans, St. Louis,

In 1682 La Salle and his party of explorers paddled from the Illinois River into the Mississippi on their way to plant the French flag at the great river's mouth. George Catlin, a specialist in portraying the Indian way of life, painted this scene in the 1840's.

Vincennes in present-day Indiana, Kaskaskia in today's Illinois. After seventy years of warring with Britain for control of the American continent, France, in 1762, secretly ceded to her ally Spain all of Louisiana west of the Mississippi and relinquished New Orleans as well. The next year, at the Treaty of Paris, victorious Britain forced France to give up all her North American possessions. Louisiana east

22

President Jefferson asked Robert Livingston, the American minister in Paris, to open talks with the French about selling at least a part of Louisiana. The great territory was bordered by the Rocky Mountains on the west and extended approximately to the present Canadian border on the north. Its eastern limit was the Mississippi River—except for New Orleans, which lay on the east side of the river. New Orleans especially was vital to the United States. All the commerce of the expanding nation west of the Appalachian Mountains traveled down rivers that led into the Mississippi, and the cargoes were finally transferred from river flatboats to ocean ships at New Orleans. Whoever owned the city could choke off the trade of Americans in the West. Buy the New Orleans region, the President instructed Livingston, or if you cannot get that, secure permanent rights to transship American goods through the port.

In the meantime, Captain Lewis went busily ahead with his preparations. At Jefferson's urging, Congress had allotted $2,500 to outfit the expedition. In March, 1803, Lewis was at the government arsenal in Harpers Ferry, Virginia, ordering knives, tomahawks, rifles made to his own design (with five hundred flints to fire them), and arranging for 176 pounds of the best gunpowder to be packed in waterproof lead canisters. He was delayed a long time by supervising construction of a cherished invention of his own. This was an iron framework for a boat,

of the Mississippi became British, and after the Revolution, part of the new United States. New Orleans and the part west, still called Louisiana, remained a possession of Spain.

Then, in 1800, Napoleon Bonaparte forced Spain to return Louisiana to France. The cession was kept secret for several months, and Spanish officials continued to administer affairs, but in 1801 the news leaked out, and Americans were very unhappy. It was bad enough to have a weak nation like Spain controlling the Louisiana country, but a strong one like France in possession could cause the United States real trouble.

23

which he named the *Experiment*. The frame, weighing ninety-nine pounds, was designed to be taken apart and packed for traveling. It would be assembled when needed, and once covered with bark and caulked with pitch, the floating *Experiment* would carry the expedition on its way.

In mid-April Lewis was in Lancaster, Pennsylvania, taking a cram course in navigation from a distinguished astronomer and buying scientific instruments. In May he moved on to Philadelphia to collect maps, gather medical supplies, buy bale upon bale of "Indian presents," and try to recruit volunteers from Army posts in the Ohio country. He got his draft instructions from the President—several pages of them. He was to take the expedition up the Missouri to its source, cross the Rocky Mountains, and then go down the recently discovered Columbia or any other river that led more directly to the Pacific. No one knew then how high or wide the Rockies were. Jefferson believed they were a single ridge of mountains and that no more than a day's travel would take the expedition from the headwaters of the Missouri to those of the Columbia.

Lewis was also instructed to note all he could about the animals, plants, minerals, soil, and climate and to learn everything possible about the Indian tribes he met on his way and the chances for future trade with them.

For this combined scientific and pioneering expedition, Captain Lewis needed a fellow officer. Someone must

An 1803 view of New Orleans salutes the addition of the city to the United States by placing an American eagle in the sunny skies. A thriving port despite its grazing cows and backdrop of forest, the town was a vital outlet for products from the expanding frontier.

This medicine chest, owned by Dr. Benjamin Rush, who was Lewis' medical advisor, contains many remedies—mostly purges—that he suggested the explorers carry with them.

liam was born and then on to the Kentucky frontier. Like most children there, William grew up with little schooling. He knew a great deal of forest lore but little grammar, and so his journals were to contain some of the most imaginative misspellings in American literature. He was also remarkably talented as a cartographer.

William was the youngest of the six boys in the large Clark family. Five, of whom the most famous was General George Rogers Clark, had been soldiers in the Revolution. William was born in 1770, too late to take part in that war, but he spent nearly eight years in the Army, fighting Indians, and was at the Battle of Fallen Timbers in 1794. The Treaty of Greenville opened up the Ohio country for American settlement the following year, and Clark traveled the Ohio and Mississippi rivers to spy out Spanish positions for General Wayne, his commander. Clark was discreet and he was capable. Ensign Meriwether Lewis, joining his rifle company in 1795, found the outgoing Lieutenant William Clark not only an able commander but a friend. The following year, however, Clark resigned because of poor health and financial problems at home, and for the last seven years he had been living on the family farm in Kentucky.

On June 19 Lewis wrote to Clark from Washington, telling him of the expedition and suggesting he take part in it. Although Lewis had been named leader of the expedition by Jefferson,

share the burdens of command, help plan the journey, and take over leadership should anything happen to him. He needed a man he could trust implicitly, preferably a friend. His thoughts at once turned to William Clark, under whom he had served on the frontier.

The President approved his suggestion. He knew the Clark family, for they too had once lived near him in Albemarle County, although they moved to eastern Virginia before Wil-

26

he courteously offered his former superior officer a part that would be equal to his own in rank and in every other way.

If therefore there is anything under those circumstances, in this enterprise, which would induce you to participate with me in it's fatiegues, it's dangers and it's honors, believe me there is no man on earth with whom I should feel equal pleasure in sharing them as with yourself; I make this communication to you with the privity of the President, who expresses an anxious wish that you would consent to join me in this enterprise.

By late July Lewis still had received no answer from Clark, and he was growing impatient to be off. Finally,

From shops around this busy Philadelphia intersection Lewis bought a gold chronometer, 130 rolls of pigtail tobacco, and $150 worth of Indian gifts: mirrors, beads, ribbon, and bells.

commission with which he proposes to furnish you is not to be considered temporary but permanent if you wish it; your situation if joined with me in this mission will in all respects be precisely such as my own. pray write to me on this subject as early as possible. and direct to me at Pittsburgh — should you feel disposed not to attatch yourself to this party in an official charac= ter, and at the same time feel a disposition to accompany me as a friend any part of the way up the Missouri I should be extreamly happy in your company, and will furnish you with every aid for your return from any point you might wish it. ——

With sincere and affectionate regard

Your friend & Humbl. Sert.

Meriwether Lewis.

Capt. William Clark.

On June 19, 1803, Lewis signed his name with a flourish (left) to a seven-page letter offering his friend Clark a part "precisely such as my own" in the projected expedition. The letter took four weeks to travel from Washington to Kentucky, and although Clark at once sat down to draft an acceptance (right), it did not reach Lewis, chafing in Pittsburgh, until July 29.

on July 26, he wrote to the President to say that he had talked to a fellow officer, Lieutenant Moses Hook, who would be happy to join the expedition, and that he meant to take Hook if he did not hear from Clark before he left Pittsburgh, where he had gone to wait for the expedition's keelboat.

But it was another month before he was able to leave Pittsburgh. The boatbuilder, who had promised that the boat would be ready on July 20, spent most of his time drunk, and despite Lewis' constant harrying, the vessel was not finally completed until August 31. In the meantime, Clark's answer arrived, and so the great adventure became the Lewis and Clark—not the Lewis and Hook—Expedition.

Actually, Clark had not delayed in answering. It was just that the mails had taken a long time going to and from his Kentucky farm. He had answered Lewis' letter the day after receiving it, first talking it over with George Rogers Clark. "This is an amence undertaking fraited with numerous dificulties," he wrote, "but my freind I can assure you that no man lives with whome I would prefur to undertake & share the Dificulties of Such a trip than yourself."

Although Lewis had promised Clark that he would be equal in rank, and the President had requested a captain's commission for him, the War Department found its own reasons for making him only a second lieutenant, a grade lower than his rank when he had resigned. It was a bitter disappointment to Clark, and to Lewis, who wrote angrily to his friend: "I think it will be best to let none of our party or any other persons know any thing about the grade, you will observe that [it] has no effect upon your compensation, which by G–d, shall be equal to my own."

Accordingly, they ignored the War Department's snub. During the long journey none of the men were ever to know that Lewis really outranked his fellow officer. Both were known as captains, and they shared the command with a lack of disagreement that has few if any equals in the history of exploration.

While the two were carrying on their slow exchange of letters, the American negotiators in Paris had been successful beyond their wildest dreams. Napoleon, with his affairs in the Americas going badly, suddenly offered all of Louisiana, a region greater in size that the entire United States of that day, for $15,000,000. It was more than the Americans were authorized to pay, but they snatched at the bargain and hoped Congress and the President would later back them up—as they did.

The agreement was dated April 30, 1803; the first ship with the official news reached the United States on July 14. This of course meant that Lewis and Clark would be traveling on American instead of foreign territory as far as the Rocky Mountains. Once across the Continental Divide, the expedition would be in the vast Oregon country, which stretched from the mountains to the Pacific and from California northward. The United States laid claim to this region, a claim based on the discovery of the Columbia River in 1792 by Captain Robert Gray, who had named the great river after his ship, the *Columbia*. Great Britain and Spain also claimed Oregon, but the United States' claim was a strong one, and the explorations of Lewis and Clark would strengthen it tremendously. Jefferson at once wrote to tell Lewis the news that would add such importance to his mission.

On the very day the long-overdue keelboat was completed, Lewis started down the Ohio with Scannon, half a dozen recruits, and a heavily laden pirogue. The river was so low that horses or oxen had to be hired at times to drag the boat across shoals. Captain Clark joined them at Louisville, Kentucky, with more volunteers, and the two friends hastened down the Ohio, purchasing another pirogue as they went. When they reached the Mississippi, they traveled up that mighty stream to the village of St. Louis and set up their winter camp opposite the mouth of the Missouri.

All winter long they worked, planned, recruited more men, and readied every detail that their experience taught them would be needed. By mid-May, 1804, therefore, the expedition was well prepared for its departure. And by early June, the members of the little "Corps of Discovery" were well on their way up the great river that was to be their road to hardship, adventure—and glory.

Crowds packed the Plaza of New Orleans on December 20, 1803, for a solemn ceremony at which the Stars and Stripes replaced the French flag, as the United States formally took possession of the Louisiana Territory.

2

UP THE WIDE MISSOURI

On May 26, 1804, Captain Meriwether Lewis made a long entry in the Corps of Discovery's orderly book, detailing the little group's organization for the long journey upstream. Most of the orders concerned the expedition's two most essential activities—getting enough to eat and maintaining a strict guard at all times.

Each of the three sergeants, John Ordway, Nathaniel Pryor, and Charles Floyd, was allotted particular duties aboard the keelboat, while the French "patroon" was made responsible for the watermen on the red pirogue, and Corporal Warfington was given command of the white pirogue's crew.

"One Sergt. shall be stationed at the helm, one in the center on the rear of the starboard locker, and one at the bow," wrote Lewis, carefully arranging that the three men should alternate duties on the keelboat each day. The sergeant at the helm was responsible for steering the boat, seeing that no

As this present-day photograph shows, parts of the Missouri have changed little since the explorers moved up its treacherous waters, mooring each night by its wooded banks.

33

baggage, "cooking utensels or loos lumber" lay about on the decks, and keeping an eye on the compass.

The sergeant at the center was to "command the guard, manage the sails, see that the men at the oars do their duty; that they come on board at a proper season in the morning, and that the boat gets under way in due time." He was also to keep his eyes peeled for topographical features that might interest his captains, "attend to the issues of sperituous liquors," post sentinels whenever the boat halted, and join the guard in reconnoitering "the forrest arround the place of landing to the distance of at least one hundred paces." At night, the distance was to be increased to one hundred fifty paces, and the watchful Lewis added to the duties a regular check on the mooring of each boat.

The sergeant at the bow was to keep a lookout for danger "either of the enimy, or obstructions" and to report "all perogues boats canoes or other craft which he may discover in the river, and all hunting camps or parties of Indians in view of which we may pass." He was provided with a setting pole, with which he could help the French bowmen, Cruzatte and Labiche, in the skilled job of maneuvering the boat through the treacherous currents and around the shifting sandbanks of the Missouri River.

In addition, each of the sergeants was ordered to keep a daily journal, and Sergeant Ordway also had the responsibility of issuing provisions and detailing men for guard duty. Each sergeant had eight men in his squad, one of whom was appointed cook, or as Lewis put it, "Superintendant of Provision," for his mess. In return for exemption from guard duty, pitching tents, and collecting firewood, the cooks had the hard task of making the expedition's rations palatable. "Lyed corn and grece" were issued one day, "the next day Poark and flour, and the day following, indian meal and poark; and in conformity to that rotiene, provisions will continue to be issued to the party untill further orders." Since cooking was allowed only when the group camped for the night, the men must have looked forward to their hot evening meal after cold, greasy snacks in the morning and at midday.

Fortunately, the banks of the river abounded with deer, turkeys, geese, squirrels and other small game, and the two horses the expedition had brought along enabled Drewyer and his fellow hunters to bring back deer, bear, and elk from the prairies that stretched as far as the eye could see in every direction. Early in June, Drewyer and John Shields were separated from the group for seven days, "depending on their gun," as Clark put it. Thereafter, the hunters did their best to return with their kill each evening. The meat that could not be cooked and eaten right away was "jerked," Indian fashion, by cutting it into thin slices that were then dried in the sun. When hard, these could be carried in a man's pouch and eaten—with much chewing—uncooked.

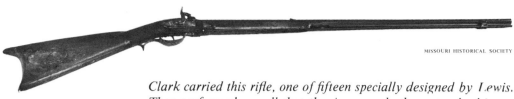

Clark carried this rifle, one of fifteen specially designed by Lewis.
They performed so well that the Army made them standard issue.

Since the expedition's stores included neither vegetables nor fruit, the men joyfully ate the fruits that grew in profusion in the woods and on the prairies: plums, raspberries, currants, grapes, and gooseberries. On at least one occasion, Clark's servant, York, swam the river to gather fresh greens and water cress for the evening meal. Even so, many of the men were sick with dysentery and boils. Clark believed the dysentery came from drinking the river water, which was milky with sediment, but the boils were probably the result of extreme exhaustion. The men were laboring from sunup to sundown in 80- to 90-degree temperatures, causing Clark to note:

Worthy of remark that the water of this river or some other cause . . . throws out a greater preposn [proportion] of Swet than I could Suppose could pass thro: the humane body Those men that do not work at all will wet a shirt in a Few minits & those who work, [the sweat] will run off in streams

The two captains, accustomed to Indians and their ways, realized the importance of impressing all those they met, whether friendly or hostile, with the expedition's military strength and constant vigilance. They ran their little party like a miniature army, with regular arms inspections and firm discipline. In the evenings, however, those men not on guard duty were able to relax around the campfire with their liquor ration or dance and sing to the music of Pierre Cruzatte's violin.

On June 29, John Collins' liking for liquor got the better of him once more. He took advantage of standing guard over the expedition's whiskey supply to help himself freely and to allow his friend Hugh Hall to do the same. A court-martial headed by Sergeant Pryor sentenced Collins to one hundred lashes, and Hall got fifty. Barely two weeks later, Alexander Willard fell asleep while on guard. Technically, this was a grave offense deserving the death penalty, but Lewis and Clark let Willard off lightly with "One hundred lashes, on his bear back, at four different times in equal proportion." By drawing out the punishment they probably hoped to make more of an impression on Willard's comrades, and if so, they succeeded. Not one member of the expedition failed in his guard duties over the months to come.

Through June and the first three weeks of July the only people they saw were white fur traders who passed them on rafts loaded high with furs and buffalo tallow bound for St. Louis. On one raft was an old French-Canadian, Pierre Dorion, who had lived for years among the Sioux tribes and spoke their language fluently. The captains were lucky in persuading him to turn back with them. Once they reached Sioux territory he would act as their interpreter. In the meantime he was a mine of information about the land they had come to explore.

On July 21 the boats reached the mouth of the wide and shallow Platte River, which flows into the Missouri not far below the present-day city of Omaha, Nebraska. They had some trouble getting through the many sand bars formed by the meeting of the rivers, but the two captains, with several men, went a mile or so up the Platte in one of the pirogues. Clark "found the Current verry rapid role-ing over Sands, passing through different Channels none of them more than five or Six feet deep."

The Oto Indians were known to live near the Platte River, so when the expedition camped the following day, Drewyer and Cruzatte were sent out to bring the Oto chiefs in for a council. While their comrades busied themselves making new oars and drying out the stores that had grown sodden on the river journey, the two leaders were "much engaged" copying out their maps and notes to send back to President Jefferson. After two days, however, Drewyer and Cruzatte returned to report that they had found

In 1834 Swiss artist Karl Bodmer made a priceless record of the still unspoiled country that Lewis and Clark had known. Here his party bivouacs on the Missouri beside a laden pirogue.

This portrait of an Oto chief, like the 1809 version of Lewis and Clark's travels that it illustrated, owes more to fancy than to fact.

only deserted villages; the entire tribe was apparently out hunting buffalo farther to the west. Once the party was on its way again, it had better luck. On July 28, Clark wrote, "G Drewyer brought in a Missourie Indian which he met with hunting in the Prarie This Indian is one of the fiew remaining of that nation, & lives with the Otteauz [Otos]."

This man, the first Indian they had met, was a grim reminder of what the opening up of this previously untouched country had done to its native inhabitants. Along with the white fur traders and explorers had come the white man's diseases. Smallpox was the worst, wiping out entire villages at a time. Even such ailments as measles, which were considered relatively minor by the whites, killed the Indians, whose bodies had no built-in resistance to them. The Missouri nation had been so reduced by disease and by wars with other tribes that the handful remaining had moved in with the Otos. And the Otos in turn had been so weakened that they had moved a few miles up the Platte River to be within the protection of the Pawnees.

The Missouri Indian was sent back with a French boatman named La Liberté to bring his people and the Oto chiefs to meet the expedition at its next stop. The following day, as they camped and waited, Clark made notes on a new animal:

Joseph Fields Killed and brought in an Anamale called by the French *Brarow*, and by the Panies [Pawnees] *Cho car tooch* this Anamale Burrows in the Ground and feeds on Flesh, (Prairie Dogs) Bugs & Vigatables his Shape & Size is like that of a Beaver, his head mouth &c. is like a Dogs with Short Ears, his Tail and Hair like that of a Ground Hog,

The beast Clark had such a hard time describing was the badger, an animal common in Europe but hitherto unknown in America.

At sunset on August 2, fourteen Oto and Missouri Indians came to the camp with a French interpreter who spoke their language, but without La Liberté. There were formal greetings and an exchange of gifts of food: roast meat, pork, flour, and meal to the Indians; "Water millions [melons]" from the Indians in return. Since this was their first Indian council, the expedition spent the night with "every man on his Guard & ready for any thing," as Clark noted.

The next morning Lewis and Clark met with the six chiefs on a bluff overlooking the river, under an awning made of the keelboat's mainsail. The captains explained that there was now a new government to take care of the Indians and gave "Some advice to them and Directions how they were to conduct themselves." Each chief made much the same answering speech: he was happy about the change in government, he hoped the captains would recommend him to the Great Father (the President), and his people were eager for more trade. Medals and presents were given out. In their twenty-one bales of "Indian presents" the captains had medals of three different grades for chiefs of differing importance.

After the gift giving, Lewis created a sensation by firing off the expedition's air gun. Air guns had been in use in England for some thirty years but were still rare in the United States. Since they could compress enough air to fire several shots and were almost as accurate as a rifle, Lewis had purchased one in Philadelphia for use should the expedition's powder run out. Even in the East the air gun had been a curiosity; on the trip west his magic weapon held the Indians spellbound.

The council ended in good feeling. Clark noted that the place of meeting was a good site for a fort and trading post because there was plenty of wood nearby, it had soil suitable for making bricks, and it was near several tribes of Indians. The captains named the place Councile Bluff. A city grew up much later on the Iowa side of the Missouri and was named Council Bluffs, but the spot where Lewis and Clark met with the chiefs was on the Nebraska side, about twenty-five miles above Council Bluffs, Iowa.

Four days later, on August 7, George Drewyer with a party of three was sent out after the missing La

The first authentic account of the party's adventures was Patrick Gass' Journal, which an enterprising schoolmaster rewrote and published in 1807. A later edition, in 1812, added such quaint illustrations as a neatly uniformed Lewis, with Clark in top hat and tailcoat, addressing a group of Indians who are barely dressed at all.

Liberté. Drewyer was also to look for Private Moses Reed, who had not been seen since he left camp on August 4 on the pretext of retrieving a knife he had left behind.

On August 18 they returned with Private Reed and a party of Oto chiefs, who had come, as requested, for further council with the captains. La Liberté had also been caught but had escaped again. Reed was court-martialed the same day and confessed:

he 'Deserted & stold a public Rifle Shot-pouch Powder & Ball' and requested we would be as favourable with him as we Could consistantly with our Oathes—which we were and only Sentenced him to run the Gantlet four times through the Party & that each man with 9 Swichies Should punish him and for him not to be considered in future as one of the Party.

In the meantime, Reed would have to remain with the expedition as a common laborer until the extra soldiers and watermen returned to St. Louis the next spring. The punishment was carried out immediately, much to the concern of the Oto chiefs, but when the white man's customs were explained to them, they "were all Satisfied with the propriety of the Sentence & was Witness to the punishment."

Once it was over, the captains talked to the Otos about their constant state of warfare with neighboring tribes, and following Jefferson's instructions, tried to interest them in living in peace. Since it was Lewis' thirtieth birthday, "the evening was closed with an extra gill [quarter-pint] of whiskey and a Dance untill 11 oClock," both of which probably made a greater impression on the Indians that all the talk about peace.

The next day Clark noted an unhappy event. "Serjeant Floyd is taken verry bad all at once with a Biliose Chorlick [colic] we attempt to relieve him without success as yet, he gets worst and we are much allarmed at his Situation, all attention to him."

Sergeant Floyd had been very ill some three weeks earlier but had apparently recovered. On the twentieth, however, his condition became so desperate that a short time after starting, the expedition halted under some bluffs. Floyd's last words were to Captain Clark: "I am going away—I want you to write me a letter." "We buried him," Clark wrote sadly in his journal, "on the top of the bluff 1/2 Mile below a Small river to which we Gave his name, he was buried with the Honors of War much lamented, a Seeder [cedar] post with the Name Sergt. C. Floyd died here 20th of august 1804 was fixed at the head of his grave."

The death of Sergeant Charles Floyd was to be the only fatality of the entire journey, an amazing record for this venture into the dangerous unknown. Nothing could have saved his life, for modern doctors believe he had an infected appendix that finally ruptured—a death sentence in those days. Two days after Floyd's death, Lewis and Clark ordered the men to

In obedience to Lewis' order that each sergeant keep a diary of "all passing occurrences . . . worthy of note," Charles Floyd recorded on July 31, 1804 (left, fourth line down): "I am verry Sick and Has ben for Somtime but have Recovered my helth again." Three weeks later he was dead, the only member of the group to perish on the journey.

nominate three candidates and elect a new sergeant. The man with the most votes was Patrick Gass, a short, barrel-chested Irishman. A first-class carpenter, he was also to prove an excellent sergeant.

That same day the boats landed at a bluff, and Captain Lewis decided to analyze some of the minerals. "By examonation this Bluff Contained Alum, Coppcras, Cobalt, Pyrites; a Alum Rock Soft & Sand Stone. Capt. Lewis in proveing the quality of those minerals was Near poisoning himself by the fumes & tast of the Cobalt . . . Copperas & alum is verry pisen," wrote Clark, adding that Lewis took a dose of salts to work off their effects.

They were now where the Missouri begins to form the southeastern border of present-day South Dakota, and there, on August 23, 1804, Joseph Fields killed the first buffalo. Millions of the huge beasts roamed the Great Plains, and until the expedition reached the Rocky Mountains, buffalo would form a large part of its daily fare. Elk was now regularly on the menu also, and the Missouri catfish were big and easy to catch. Sergeant Gass noted in his journal that nine of the catfish caught one day would together have weighed about three hundred pounds.

By August 25 they were nearing the country of the Yankton Sioux, one of the tribes of the powerful Sioux nation, and following Dorion's advice, they began setting the prairie grass afire as a signal to call the Indians to a council. At the junction of the James River and the Missouri they finally met three Indians, who told them a village of Yankton Sioux was nearby. Dorion and two of the men went to make arrangements for a meeting and were hospitably entertained by the villagers with a dinner of dog meat, which they found delicious. Five chiefs and about seventy men and boys accompanied them back to the boats, and a council was arranged for the next day.

The Sioux were a warlike people who bullied other tribes and demanded outrageously high payments from traders going up the Missouri. Even while the expedition was being planned, Lewis and Clark had feared that the Sioux would not permit them to pass through their territory. Much depended on their interpreter's ability

and the impression they and their party made during the talks.

The decisive meeting took place on August 30, under a large oak tree. The American flag, with its fifteen stars and fifteen stripes, flew nearby. The usual speech from Lewis was interpreted by Dorion: the Sioux were now subject to a new government and a new Great Father who would send traders to provide them with all they needed. In the meantime, Lewis said, he expected the Indians to remain at peace with their neighbors. There were gifts: for the leading chief a flag, a medal, some wampum, and a richly laced army uniform with a cocked hat and red feather, and for the lesser

JOHN J. AUDUBON, *The Quadrupeds of North America,* 1851

Prairie dogs, which the explorers called barking squirrels, were later engraved by Audubon.

42

chiefs, tobacco, medals, and clothing. That night the Indians danced until late, and the watching Americans rewarded them by throwing gifts of knives, tobacco, bells, and colored binding into the circle of dancers.

The next day the chiefs "arranged themselves in a row with elligent pipes of peace all pointing to our Seets." Although they were friendly, their response was mostly complaints about their poverty and how niggardly the captains' gifts of the day before had been. They wanted more gunpowder and bullets and "a little Milk"—the Indian term for whiskey was "milk of Great Father."

The captains put them off with promises, and Dorion offered to try to arrange a peace between the various Sioux tribes and their neighbors. After equipping him with gifts to aid in this difficult task, Lewis and Clark left him behind and continued their journey. They were thankful to have had no trouble with the Yankton Sioux, although still to be faced up-river were the warlike Teton Sioux.

On September 5 the party saw their first pronghorn antelope, an animal new to American science. Only two days later they met another new creature. On shore they discovered an area of about four acres with many holes, each the home of a small furry animal. Some five barrels of water were not enough to fill one of the holes but did dislodge the bedraggled owner, which was captured. The men dug down another hole for six feet and then, poking with a pole, found they had not dug halfway to the bottom. The creatures were prairie dogs.

On a hill they found the backbone of a petrified "fish," forty-five feet long, and knowing President Jefferson's interest in such things, took a few of the bones for him. In fact, of course, the bones belonged not to a fish but to a prehistoric dinosaur.

As they proceeded, trees along the river grew scarce, but the animals were, if anything, more numerous. Lewis spent one day ashore to "view the interior of the country" and was quite overcome by the richness of this wilderness and the "immence herds of Buffaloe, deer Elk and Antelopes. . . ." They shot a pelican. Grouse were abundant; porcupines were common. In mid-September they killed one of the bushy-tailed, howling animals they had been calling gray foxes and found it was really a small species of wolf. Its mournful cry in the night still sounds in the West; we know the beast as the coyote.

On September 21 the expedition had a very narrow escape, not from hostile Indians but from the Missouri itself. Clark's account makes light of his own presence of mind, which saved them all:

At half past one o'clock this morning the Sand bar on which we Camped began to under mind and give way which allarmed the Serjeant on Guard, the motion of the boat awakened me; I got up & by the light of the moon observed that the Sand had given away both above and below

our Camp & was falling in fast. I ordered
all hands on as quick as possible &
pushed off, we had pushed off but a few
minits before the bank under which the
Boat & perogus lay give way, which
would Certainly have Sunk both Perogues,
by the time we made the ops.ᵈ Shore our
Camp fell in,

Two days later, they finally came
across the Teton Sioux. Three boys
swam out to the men and told them
that two large parties of Teton were
camped upriver where the next river
entered the Missouri—the point at
which Pierre, South Dakota, now
stands. The captains gave the lads tobacco to take to their chiefs, and also
the message that they would meet with
the chiefs the next day.

They did not reach the Sioux the
following day. But John Colter came
in from hunting to report that Indians
had stolen his horse, one of the precious two without which the expedition could not hunt effectively. Shortly
after, five Sioux were seen on shore,
and the expedition stopped a safe distance from the bank. The captains
called out to the Indians that the horse
had been sent by the Great Father, the
President, for their chief (they were
stretching the truth) and that they
"would not Speek to them untill the
horse was returned . . . again."

The next day they anchored to prepare for a formal meeting. When the
Teton Sioux party arrived from their
camp nearby, their three chiefs were
accompanied by some fifty or sixty
warriors, and the men were on their

44

The oldest painted buffalo hide in existence, this ceremonial robe was sent by the captains to President Jefferson in 1805. It depicts an attack on the Mandans by the Sioux and Arikaras, eight years before the expedition tried to make a lasting peace between the tribes.

guard as they paraded to welcome them. Now the captains felt the absence of Dorion. The French waterman whom they had to use as interpreter knew so little Sioux that Lewis was obliged to shorten his usual speech. The gift giving that followed was more successful, but when the chiefs were invited aboard the keelboat to be shown the air gun and "such Curiossities," the trouble the captains had feared began.

We gave them 1/4 a glass of whiskey which they appeared to be verry fond of, Sucked the bottle after it was out & Soon began to be troublesom, one the 2d Cheif assumeing Drunkness, as a Cloake for his rascally intentions

Clark and five men took the chiefs ashore in a pirogue, but as soon as they landed, three warriors seized the cable so the boat could not return.

The 2d Chief was verry insolent both in words & justures (pretended Drunkenness & staggered up against me) declareing I should not go on, Stateing he had not received presents sufficient from us, his justures were of Such a personal nature I felt My self Compeled to Draw my Sword (and Made a Signal to the boat to prepare for action) . . . I felt My Self warm & Spoke in verry positive terms.

It was a tense moment. Captain Lewis had all his men under arms while the keelboat's swivel guns kept the Indians covered. Captain Clark was already on shore, surrounded by menacing warriors, but he managed to send the pirogue back for help. Twelve men swarmed into it and

rowed ashore to join him. The Sioux had never met this kind of resistance before, and the leading chief, Black Buffalo, told his men to draw back.

Captain Clark did not want to make lasting enemies. He offered to shake hands with Black Buffalo and the second chief, named The Partisan, but both refused. When Clark climbed on board the pirogue, however, Black Buffalo and the third chief followed, with two warriors, and the captain brought all four on board the keelboat. The party anchored about a mile away, off an island that they sourly named "bad humered Island."

The four Indians remained with them all night, and in the morning the chiefs, who seemed more friendly, asked the captains to let their women and children see the boats. Eager to

Though imaginary, this Sioux warrior, by the artist who depicted the Oto chief on page 38, radiates the fierce pride of the real tribe.

win the friendship of the Sioux if they could, Lewis and Clark took the boats close to the shore, and the entire village crowded down to the river's edge to see them. The captains also gave in to the urging of the Sioux to be their guests at a dance that night.

When the time came, first Clark and then Lewis was met by ten young men, placed on a richly painted buffalo robe, and carried in state to a large round council house covered with hides. The Indians smoked the peace pipe with their guests and with many ceremonies offered them four hundred pounds of buffalo meat as a gift. Then they feasted—on pemmican, a root called the ground potato, and dog meat. Clark thought the pemmican and ground potato good but he "eat little of dog." This was one of the very few things on which he disagreed with Lewis, who, like virtually every other expedition member, came to consider dog meat delicious. Clark never did get to like it.

After dinner the dancing began, to the music of skin drums and rattles made of antelope hoofs tied to long sticks. About midnight Lewis and Clark made their excuses and returned to the boat. They were accompanied by four chiefs who stayed the night with them as self-invited guests.

The next evening Lewis and Clark attended another dance, and when they returned, The Partisan and a warrior went with them. The pirogue taking them from shore to the anchored keelboat was being handled by an in-

Clark's "Baling Invoice of Sundries for Indian Presents" lists the contents of one of the bales of gifts intended for chiefs along the way. Two chief's coats, with plumed hats, go to the principal chief; lesser leaders get "Scarlet Leggins" and "Britch Clouts."

experienced man, and in coming alongside the boat, he brought the pirogue against the anchor cable and snapped it. The keelboat began drifting, and Clark was forced

to order in a loud voice all hands up & at their ores, my preemptry order to the men and the bustle of their getting to their ores allarmd [The Partisan, who] hollowaed & allarmed the Camp or Town

47

informing them that the Mahars [Omahas] was about attacking us. In about 10 minits the bank was lined with men armed the 1st. Cheif at their head,

Despite the shouting about the Omahas, the captains suspected that the Sioux were afraid the expedition was trying to leave and had raised a false alarm to stop it. That guess was confirmed by Pierre Cruzatte, who spoke the Omaha language. There were in the village a number of Omaha captives taken by the Sioux on a recent raid, and they had managed to warn Cruzatte that the Sioux planned to stop the expedition if they could.

"The Plains of this countrey are covered with a Leek green Grass," wrote Clark, *moved to question why it should "be enjoyed by nothing but the Buffalo Elk Deer & Bear in which it abounds & Savage Indians." In 1847, H. G. Hine painted the untamed prairie before it vanished forever.*

With its anchor lost, the keelboat had to tie up to the bank, exposed to possible attacks, and Lewis and Clark spent a sleepless night. In the morning a group of Indians crowded onto the boat, and the captains had great difficulty getting them to go ashore. When finally all but Black Buffalo, the principal chief, were gone and everything

48

was made ready to cast off, there was fresh trouble: several warriors were sitting on the mooring rope. The exasperated commanders made ready to shoot, but Clark managed to touch the pride of Black Buffalo by implying that he had no control over his men. Whereupon ". . . he jurked the rope from them and handed it to the bowsman we then Set out under a Breeze from the S.E."

In fact, it appears that the leading chief, Black Buffalo, was inclined to be friendly, although he did not dare show it too openly before The Partisan, the second chief, who hated whites and was behind all the trouble. It was probably to prevent any further mishaps that Black Buffalo remained with the party as they proceeded upriver. Several Teton Sioux on the banks invited them to come ashore, but Lewis and Clark sensibly refused, sending them tobacco and good advice instead. On the second day the keelboat hit a log and heeled over so far that she almost capsized. This was too much for Black Buffalo, who insisted on being put ashore. In any case, he said, the expedition was now past Teton Sioux territory and would have no more trouble.

3

INTO THE GREAT UNKNOWN

Once they left the country of the Teton Sioux, Lewis and Clark journeyed on up the Missouri without further hindrance from Indians. The channels between the sand bars were becoming shallower each day, but the captains managed to lighten the keelboat by transferring some of their stores to the pirogues. Yet the men still had to strain with ropes and poles to get the heavy boat through the shoaling water—and the weather was turning colder each day.

As early as September 16, Clark had issued a flannel shirt to each man, and on October 5 they woke to find frost on the ground. For some time they had been passing the ruins of long-deserted villages. These had once been peopled by the Arikara Indians. White men had brought smallpox, the warrior Sioux had come, and the surviving Arikaras had moved upriver for greater safety.

On October 8 the Corps of Discovery reached the first occupied Arikara village and were fortunate in finding two French traders who could serve as interpreters. The Arikaras were not tepee-dwelling nomads like the Sioux.

They lived in houses with rounded roofs made of willow branches covered with a layer of mud. Each village of these domed houses was surrounded by a rough picketed fence, and within its protective wall the Arikaras cultivated beans, squash, pumpkins, and tobacco, supplementing their diet by going out on the prairie from time to time to hunt buffalo.

For two days Lewis and Clark met in council with the Indians, making their speeches about the new government and going through the rest of the now-familiar routine. The Arikaras, unlike the Tetons, seemed ready to be friendly, but once they discovered Clark's Negro slave, York, they became more interested in him than in anything else. They had seen red men and white men but never a man with black skin. York, who had a great deal of the actor in him, awed

The Mandans, with whom the party spent the winter of 1804–05, were an artistic, friendly tribe. George Catlin, who painted Chief Four Bears (right) in 1832, called the handsome chief one of "Nature's noblemen."

the Indians with feats of strength and told them how he had been a wild animal "and lived upon people" until caught and tamed by Clark. His master felt he overdid it somewhat:

Those Indians wer much astonished at my Servent, they never Saw a black man before, all flocked around him & examind him from top to toe, he Carried on the joke and made himself more turribal than we wished him to doe.

On October 11 and 12 captains Lewis and Clark visited the other two Arikara villages—three were all that remained of what were said to have been ten strong bands before the ravages of smallpox and the Sioux. Then the expedition pushed off again, for Lewis was eager to reach the Mandan Indians, next upriver, before the true

winter cold set in. Much to their satisfaction, their talk about peace had already borne fruit. An Arikara chief traveled with them as an ambassador of good will to the Mandans, with whom the Arikaras were then at war.

On October 14 they stopped on a sand bar for an unpleasant duty. The day before, Private John Newman had been court-martialed for insubordination, and now he was given seventy-five lashes. The Arikara chief, like the Otos, was distressed at the sight, but when Clark explained that examples were necessary, the chief said that he made examples too—by killing offenders. The captains had an equally effective method, however. The unlucky Newman was also separated from the Army and sentenced to be sent back down-river with the re-

WILLIAM FISHER, *An Interesting Account* . . . , 1813: NEW YORK PUBLIC LIBRARY

An 1813 "account" of the expedition enticed readers with such wildly inaccurate illustrations as this view of Indian tepees on the Washita—a river Lewis and Clark never visited.

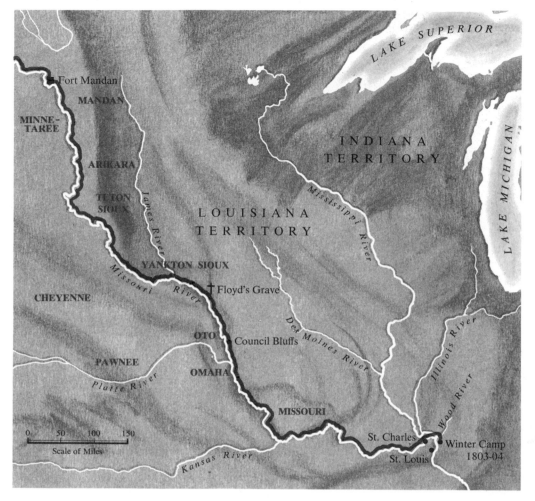

The expedition averaged barely fifteen miles a day as they heaved their three boats against the swift current of the winding Missouri. Leaving their winter camp (right) on May 14, 1804, they journeyed northwest, reaching the Mandans in late October, and began building Fort Mandan (top left) in November. In six months they had traveled sixteen hundred miles.

turning party in the spring. It was a hard decision. Newman begged to be allowed to remain with the expedition, and he worked especially hard during the winter to earn forgiveness. Lewis, however, felt he must remain firm and dispatched both Newman and Reed to St. Louis the next year.

The example seemed to have good effect. There was no more trouble. The high-spirited young men were willing to risk a whipping but would take no chances of being sent home.

The weather grew colder. Several of the men came down with rheumatism. Clark was immobilized by vio-

Lewis preserved a mass of specimens, describing them in detail in case they were spoiled. C. W. Peale drew this horned toad from one of the few to reach Washington.

lent neck spasms until Lewis "applied a hot Stone raped in flannel, which gave me some temporey ease."

On October 24 a few flakes of snow floated down in the morning, and that same day they met their first Mandans, a hunting party led by one of the principal chiefs. The Mandans were a tribe much more advanced than most. Sixty-six years earlier, the French explorer La Vérendrye, who was the first white man to visit them, had found the Mandans living in nine villages sixty miles down the river, about where Bismarck, North Dakota, now stands. But smallpox had wiped out most of them, and marauding Sioux tribes had driven those who survived farther up the Missouri.

On October 27 the expedition reached the two remaining Mandan villages. Close by were three villages of the Minnetaree, or Hidatsa, a tribe whom the French called *Gros Ventres*, meaning "Big Bellies." Both Mandans and Minnetarees lived in round, earth-covered lodges like those of the Arikaras down-river. Like the Arikaras, they were farming peoples, but from living close to Canada they had grown accustomed to trading with white men.

The Mandan villages had been the expedition's autumn destination from the beginning, and now the captains chose for their winter camp a wooded place about three miles down-river from the lower village. On November 3 the men began building cabins for their fort, and the next day Clark noted in his journal that "a Mr. Chaubonie, interpeter for the Gross Ventre nation Came to See us . . . this man wished to hire as an interpiter." The expedition would see much more of this man, Toussaint Charbonneau.

After two weeks of hard work in the cottonwood groves, the cabins were completed, and the party moved in on November 20. There were two rows of four cabins, each one fourteen feet square, built at right angles to each other to form two sides of a triangle. A palisade of posts joined the open base of the triangle, and two storerooms filled in its apex. This structure, named Fort Mandan, proudly flew the American flag that winter of 1804–05 as the westernmost military outpost of the United States.

Lewis and Clark computed that they had traveled sixteen hundred miles since they left the Mississippi.

It was a busy winter. A surprising amount of traffic passed through and around the Mandan villages. Pawnees and Cheyennes visited from far to the south. Arikaras arrived from downriver, and Assiniboins came from the north through the bitter cold. Traders from the British posts on the Assiniboine River in Canada, some eight days' travel to the north, came and left as casually as though they were Boston merchants making routine business trips through New England rather than men setting out on journeys over wind-swept plains in tem-

MAXIMILIAN, *Travels in the Interior* . . . , 1834: YALE UNIVERSITY LIBRARY

In 1833 Bodmer, like Lewis and Clark before him, wintered near the lower Mandan village. His view shows earthen-mound houses dominating the Missouri from a forty-foot cliff. Beneath it, squaws haul wood ashore in round bullboats made of buffalo hide on willow frames.

At Fort Mandan the captains worked on the preparation of a map showing the continent west of the Mississippi, based on "the Authorities of the best informed travellers." As this 1806 copy shows, the map is recognizable where they used their own records, but Indian hearsay misled them into placing the still-unexplored Rockies far too close to the Pacific.

56

peratures sometimes far below zero.

The weather was colder than any the party had yet experienced. In mid-December the thermometer plunged to 45 degrees below zero. The next day was not quite so cold— only 32 degrees below at sunrise—but Clark noted: "Sent out 7 men to hunt for the Buffalow they found the weather too cold & returned."

At Christmas, the men had a celebration, but the Indians, as Sergeant Ordway explained in his diary, were excluded:

We fired the Swivels at day break & each man fired one round. our officers Gave the party a drink of Taffe [rum]. we had the Best to eat that could be had, & continued firing dancing & frolicking dureing the whole day. the Savages did not Trouble us as we had requested them not to come as it was a great medician day with us.

New Year's Day was a different story. Then Lewis and Clark permitted sixteen of the men to visit the nearest Mandan village in the morning, carrying with them "a fiddle & a Tambereen & a Sounden horn." Some time later Clark walked to the village. He found the Indians "much pleased at the Danceing of our men, I ordered my black Servent to Dance which amused the Croud Verry much, and Somewhat astonished them, that So large a man should be active &c."

But the two holidays were only brief interludes. There was much work to be done. Hunters went out each day the weather made it possible. The captains carefully questioned Indians and

Lewis and Clark sent Jefferson a Mandan bow with a decorated quiver full of Indian tobacco seeds. While visiting the Mandans, Bodmer painted a similar bow and a quiver with traditional ornamentation. Only three years later a sudden smallpox epidemic destroyed the Mandans and their civilization.

Huddled in skins to protect them from the subzero cold, Indians stream on foot or on ponyback across the frozen Missouri to the Mandan village. By 1834, as Bodmer's painting shows, the stockade of Fort Clark (left), a military and trading post named for the explorer, had joined the village on its cliff.

traders about the tribes, their customs, where they might be found, and especially about the topographical features of the unknown country ahead of them. They gathered a large amount of information to be sent back to the President when they left in the spring.

As the only people with any medical knowledge, the two officers were also kept busy treating their own men and the Indians who came for help. It was not just a case of ointments and tonics. "I bleed the man with the Plurisy to day & Swet him," Clark noted one day. "Capt. Lewis took off the Toes of one foot of the Boy who got frost bit Some time ago."

Lewis was also called to help in a case he knew nothing about. Toussaint Charbonneau, the Canadian who had come to them in early November asking for work, had been hired as an interpreter. Charbonneau, a man of forty-five, had been living with the Minnetarees for about five years and spoke their difficult language quite well. During his stay he had purchased two young "wives," Shoshoni girls less than half his age, who had been captured by a Minnetaree war party in the foothills of the Rockies. On February 11 the younger of the two, the sixteen-year-old Sacagawea, was in labor with her first baby and having a difficult time. Lewis' brief training in medicine and first aid had not prepared him for this. When a trader mentioned that a rattlesnake's rattle never failed in such cases, Lewis found one among his specimens and gave it to him. Crumbling some into a cup of water, the trader made Sacagawea drink it—and shortly afterward, whether helped by the rattle or not, she gave birth to a healthy boy. Both Sacagawea (whose name means "Bird Woman") and her baby son would accompany Lewis and Clark to the Pacific and back.

On April 7, 1805, the expedition left its winter camp. It was now traveling in the two pirogues and in six canoes built by the men out of cottonwood timber and coated with pitch to make them waterproof. Enlistments from the return party had replaced the loss of Sergeant Floyd and the two court-martialed men, and Charbonneau and his family had been added. The expedition now numbered thirty-three, including Sacagawea's two-month-old baby, who traveled in a papoose board strapped to her back.

That same day the return party departed down-river in the keelboat, carrying nine boxes of scientific specimens for the President, including a live prairie dog and four live magpies. Even more valuable, however, were the mass of reports and the detailed map that the two captains had labored all winter to compile.

While Clark took their little fleet by water to the first camp, Lewis enjoyed a ramble on the bank and later confided in his journal:

We were now about to penetrate a country at least two thousand miles in width, on which the foot of civilized man had never trodden; the good or evil it had in store for us was for experiment yet to determine, and these little vessells contained every article by which we were to expect to subsist or defend ourselves. however . . . enterta[in]ing as I do, the most confident hope of succeeding in a voyage which had formed a da[r]ling project of mine for the last ten years, I could but esteem this moment of my departure as among the most happy of my life.

The geese were flying north as the expedition started, and cottonwood, elm, and maple buds were swelling. On April 9 Clark noted that flowers were blooming on the prairie, and that same day a less pleasant sign of spring appeared. Mosquitoes were out and were troublesome.

For a while, day followed day uneventfully. Then there was a close brush with disaster on April 13 when a sudden squall struck the white pirogue as it was moving along under sail. The boat heeled over, and Charbonneau, at the helm, became panicky and turned it broadside to the wind. The pirogue came within an eyelash of capsizing. The wind eased for a moment, however, and Lewis ordered Drewyer to take the helm. Not only were records, medicine, and trade goods jeopardized, but the lives of several men and of Sacagawea and her baby—none of whom could swim— had been imperiled. It was not the only time Charbonneau's clumsiness would cause trouble.

On April 26 the expedition reached the wide mouth of the Yellowstone River, and Captain Lewis and Joseph Fields spent the day exploring the area. The party camped for the night close to the junction of the two great rivers, "all in good health, and much pleased at having arrived at this long wished for spot." To add to the pleasure, the captains ordered a liquor ration for each man. "This soon produced the fiddle, and they spent the evening with much hilarity, singing & dancing, and seemed as perfectly to forget their past toils, as they appeared regardless of those to come," Lewis noted in his diary.

Shortly afterward, they crossed into the present state of Montana, and three days later they met their first grizzly bears—two of them at once. Lewis and another man both fired. One wounded animal fled; the other pursued Lewis but was so badly hurt that the captain had a chance to reload his gun and kill the animal. "In the hands of skillfull riflemen they are by no means as formidable or dangerous as they have been represented," he wrote, rather boastfully. Later he was to learn how lucky they had been.

A cold snap in early May froze the water on the oars, and ice was a quarter inch thick in the kettle when they awoke. Clark noted "a verry extraodernarey climate, to behold the trees Green & flowers spred on the plain, & Snow an inch deep." By now they were in territory where no white man had ever stepped, and they kept on the lookout for Indians. But although they were constantly passing deserted Indian hunting camps, they encountered none of their inhabitants.

For the Indians of the Upper Missouri life revolved around the buffalo. They devised elaborate rituals to attract the vast herds that were the main source of food and clothing. In battle each warrior used a shield of toughened buffalo hide painted with a design he believed would give him supernatural power. Often, as on these Arikara shields, the magical picture incorporated a buffalo.

Bodmer's 1833 painting of the junction of the Missouri and the Yellowstone magnificently conveys the isolation and grandeur of the scene, although by then a fur-trading fort was doing brisk business from the "long wished for spot" where the 1805 expedition spent a merry evening drinking and dancing.

On May 5 Clark and Drewyer killed a huge grizzly bear. "It was a most tremendious looking anamal," wrote Lewis, measuring more than eight and a half feet from the tip of its nose to its hind feet. Captain Clark estimated that it weighed five hundred pounds, but Lewis thought it must be at least six hundred pounds.

The best warning of the dangers of grizzly-bear hunting with muzzle-loading rifles came a few days later when six men, "all good hunters," came on one of the huge beasts lying not far from the river. Four men fired, and all the shots hit the bear, two of them piercing the animal's lungs. Infuriated, it immediately charged the hunters. The two who had held their fire now shot. Both bullets hit the bear, and one broke its shoulder, but the beast's pace barely slowed for an instant. With no time to reload their clumsy guns, the entire party ran for their lives. Two men fled in a canoe, and four hid in the bushes and fired as fast as they could load. The bear found two of them, and they had to throw themselves over a twenty-foot cliff into the river to escape. Leaping after them, the bear had almost caught the hindermost when one of the men on shore shot the enraged beast through the head. When they finally skinned the great animal, they found that eight bullets had passed through it in different directions.

The same day Charbonneau nearly ruined the expedition a second time. Once again he was at the helm of the white pirogue, under sail, when a squall struck the craft. Just as he had a month before, he turned it the wrong way as it heeled over. Lewis and Clark were both on shore and too far away to help or to be heard by the men on the pirogue. As Lewis described it:

Such was their confusion and consternation at this moment, that they suffered the perogue to lye on her side for half a minute before they took the sail in. The perogue then wrighted but had filled within an inch of the gunwals; Charbono still crying to his god for mercy, had not yet recollected the rudder, nor could the repeated orders of the Bowsman, Cruzat, bring him to his recollection untill he threatend to shoot him instantly if he did

Without intending to be funny, an 1813 engraving presents an odd version of one of the party's many terrifying encounters with infuriated grizzlies. A uniformed expedition member runs to seek refuge in a river as an interested bear lumbers after him.

not take hold of the rudder and do his duty.

Two men grabbed kettles and bailed out enough water to keep the boat afloat until it was rowed ashore. Lewis wrote of the incident with great feeling, for the pirogue contained "almost every article indispensibly necessary to further the views, or insure the success of the enterpize in which we are now launched to the distance of 2200 miles." He noted, however, that while Sacagawea's spouse had been frozen with fear, she had "caught and preserved most of the light articles which were washed overboard."

By May 17 the men had to tow the pirogues. "We employed the toe line the greater part of the day; the banks were firm and shore boald [bare] which favoured the uce of the cord." The landscape was becoming much more hilly, and on May 26 Lewis climbed a height and "beheld the

Rocky Mountains for the first time."
He felt a surge of elation at the sight
of the distant snow-covered peaks
glistening in the sun, both at "finding
myself so near the head of the heretofore conceived boundless Missouri"
and at reflecting "on the difficulties
which this snowey barrier would most
probably throw in my way to the
Pacific, and the sufferings and hard-
ships of myself and party in thim. . . ."

Three days later a lone buffalo
came charging through their camp in
the middle of the night and nearly put
an end to the entire expedition. Ignor-
ing the sentry's frantic attempts to
scare him away, the buffalo made
straight for the captains' tent, which
was surrounded by rows of sleeping
men. Scannon saved the day, however, by setting up a furious barking.

*Their first sight of the Rockies was a moment
filled with emotion for both captains. This
view of what they called "the Shining Mountains" was made fifteen years later by the
next official expedition to visit the area.*

The buffalo suddenly swerved to one
side and made off into the night, missing a row of sleepers by inches and
"leaving us . . . all in an uproar with
our guns in o[u]r hands, enquiring of
each other the ca[u]se of the alarm,"
Lewis noted ruefully.

That day they passed a 120-foot
cliff over which Indians had stam-
peded a buffalo herd. At least a hundred rotting carcasses lay at the base
of the precipice by the river's edge,
and the wolves were having a field
day. Lewis noted in his journal that
tribes on the Missouri regularly destroyed vast herds of buffalo by decoy-

ing them to a precipice and then stampeding them over the side in a frantic drive. It was an easy means of getting plenty of buffalo beef—except for the decoy. Disguised in a buffalo hide, this man ran in front of a herd until he reached the cliff and then, if he was lucky, jumped aside.

On May 31 the men spent much of the day up to their armpits in the water towing the boats along. They were passing through an area of constant riffles and rocky bars, and the river bluffs were too close and too slippery to allow them a foothold. There was one consolation, however; the cliffs had been worn by erosion "into a thousand grotesque figures, which with the help of a little immagination . . . are made to represent eligant ranges of lofty freestone buildings, having their parapets well stocked with statuary [and] collumns of various sculpture," wrote Lewis, marveling.

Two days later they arrived at an unexpected forking of the river into two large streams. Most of the men were certain the northern branch was the right one because it was brown and muddy like the Missouri they had been following so long. But both the captains believed that the south fork, flowing clear over a bed of stones, was the correct one, since it had obviously come recently from a mountain source. No one's mind was changed

Visiting the West in 1837, Alfred Jacob Miller graphically recorded how the Indians hunted buffalo by stampeding the near-sighted beasts over a steep cliff. Beneath some precipices regularly used in this way the first four feet of soil is still solid bone and blood meal, the harvest of thousands of carcasses heedlessly left to rot once their valued tongues and humps had been removed.

after Lewis led a party up the north branch, and Clark one up the south fork for two or three days. Lewis named the north fork the Marias River, after his cousin, whose "celestial virtues and amiable qualifications" he much admired. When the two captains returned, they remained confident that the south fork was the true continuation of the Missouri.

Artist Charles Willson Peale, an enthusiastic amateur naturalist, made these drawings in 1806 from Lewis' specimens of a mountain quail (top) and a woodpecker. Lewis had intended them to illustrate his projected book on the expedition, but it was never published, and neither were the drawings.

[The men] said very cheerfully that they were ready to follow us any wher we thought proper to direct but that they still thought that the other was the river and that they were affraid that the South fork would soon termineate in the mountains and leave us at a great distance from the Columbia.

Although this was in no way a challenge to their leadership, the captains democratically humored the men: Lewis would take a party and push ahead by land until he reached the waterfalls that the Indians at Fort Mandan had said they would find on the Missouri River.

To lighten the load and provide more hands to work the oars and towlines, the captains decided to leave the red pirogue and all the heavy supplies that could be spared at the fork of the rivers. Cruzatte organized the making of a cache. First he carefully removed a circle of sod about twenty inches in diameter. A hole was dug straight down about a foot, then was gradually widened to make an area six or seven feet deep and shaped like a kettle. The hole was floored with three or four inches of dry sticks covered with dry grass, and the goods were piled in, with care taken to keep them from contact with the earth walls. Once the hole was almost full, the supplies were covered with hides, the rest of the space filled up with earth, and the sod carefully replaced on the top. In a well-made cache there would be no sign after a few days that the ground had ever been disturbed, and

THE HUNTINGTON LIBRARY, SAN MARINO, CALIFORNIA

Lewis sketched the Great Falls of the Missouri as a guide to "some abler pencil" in drawing it later. This contemporary engraving may perhaps have been based on his rough sketch.

the goods would keep safe for months, or in some cases, for years.

Excess food, salt, scientific specimens, blacksmith tools, part of the powder and lead, and other extra baggage were hidden in two of these caches. The red pirogue was hauled up onto a small island in the Marias River and firmly lashed to trees to prevent its being swept away by floods. Although the captains were hoping that at least some of the party would be able to take ship from the Columbia and go back around the world, they prepared with their usual care for a return trip that would follow their outgoing route.

On June 11 Lewis with four men set off by land, leaving Clark and the rest of the party to follow the endless bends of the Missouri by boat. On their third day out, Lewis and his party heard the distant roar of falling water and soon saw ahead of them a column of rising spray that looked like smoke. When they reached the waterfall, Lewis found it a majestic sight, some three hundred yards wide, by his first estimate, and eighty feet high (it was actually ninety or more). A third of it fell in a smooth transparent sheet and the rest was broken up by projecting rocks into bounding, hurtling jets of water.

There was no doubt now that they were on the right river, for the Indians at Fort Mandan had told them that there was a series of mighty waterfalls on the river that led to the mountains. Their new discovery, the Great Falls

69

of the Missouri, was the highest of a long series of falls and rapids extending over a ten-mile stretch of the river. Lewis celebrated "the grandest sight I ever beheld" with an excellent dinner and wrote cheerfully in his journal: "My fare is really sumptuous this evening; buffaloe's humps, tongues and marrowbones, fine trout parched meal pepper and salt, and a good appetite; the last is not considered the least of the luxuries."

Next morning he dispatched Joseph Fields to carry the good news back to Clark, who was proceeding slowly with his own problems. He had "two men with the Tooth ake 2 with Tumers [boils], & one man with a Tumor & a slight fever." Sacagawea, who had been taken sick at the Marias River fork, was now critically ill. Clark had bled her and done everything else he knew. Once Clark's party reached the falls, Lewis took over with doses of quinine and opium. Water from a nearby sulphur spring helped miraculously; Sacagawea began to recover at once and was soon demanding all the broiled buffalo "and rich soope of the same meat" that Lewis would give her.

The cascades and rapids of the Great Falls area meant eighteen miles of difficult portaging over rough ground covered with cactus. The captains ordered each man to go rigorously through his baggage and winnow out everything that could be spared. Another cache was made at the foot of the portage, and the white

Rainbow Falls (above), one of the ten-mile series of cascades and falls in the Great Falls area, still justifies Lewis' ecstatic description of it as "singularly beautiful."

pirogue hidden in the willows. Its mast was cut up to furnish axles for a pair of rough four-wheeled trucks on which they could draw the canoes. After a long search the men found a cottonwood tree about twenty-two inches in diameter from which they cut rounds for wheels. Lewis did not think they could have found another of like size within twenty miles.

The portage was heartbreaking work. Although the men had double-

70

soled their moccasins against the prickly-pear cactus, many of the spines penetrated, and the uneven earth hurt their feet. They had to catch at rocks and clumps of grass to help haul the trucks up the slopes, and so close to exhaustion were they that at the brief rests they would fall asleep in a moment.

Frequent storms made the going muddy and even more difficult. An especially violent one on June 29 brought hail so fierce that it knocked down and bloodied some of the men. Clark was out with Sacagawea, the baby, Charbonneau, and York when the storm struck, and they took shelter in a ravine under an overhanging rock. "The rain fell like one voley of water falling from the heavens and gave us time only to get out of the way of a torrent of water which was Pore-ing down the hill . . . with emence force tareing everything before it take-ing with it large rocks & mud," as Clark described it later. Pushing Saca-gawea in front of him, while she fran-tically clutched the baby, Clark scrambled out just before fifteen feet of water raced over the spot where they had been. A number of objects were lost, including Clark's umbrella and Sacagawea's papoose board. The next day, when the men searched the ravine, they almost miraculously found the one article that was indis-pensable: the expedition's large com-pass, the only large one they had.

The first load to come up the portage was the iron framework of Lewis' boat, the *Experiment*. Now at last was the time to put it to the test. Since there was no suitable bark in the area to cover its frame, Lewis organ-ized a body of hunters to bring in elk and buffalo skins to serve instead. But the leather thongs used to sew the hide covering to the frame left holes larger than Lewis had expected, and there were no evergreen trees from which to make pitch for caulking the leaks. The charcoal-and-tallow mixture he sub-stituted would not stick to the hides, and as a result, the *Experiment* leaked like a sieve. "I therefore relinquished all further hope of my favorite boat," wrote Lewis sadly. He ordered it to be taken apart, the frame was buried, and its rusty remains are undoubtedly there in Montana yet.

In a drawing by Charles M. Russell, a cow-boy who became Montana's most famous artist, Charbonneau (left) clasps Sacaga-wea's hand as Clark pushes mother and baby ahead of him out of a flooded ravine.

71

4

CROSSING THE DIVIDE

With Meriwether Lewis' precious boat a failure, Captain Clark sent a party in search of timber for two dugout canoes to take the *Experiment*'s place. In the country around the Great Falls only the river banks were wooded, and there were very few trees of any size. The woodcutters kept breaking their axe handles and having to stop to whittle out new ones. On one memorable day, four men broke thirteen handles. A month had passed since they had left the Marias River, and Lewis was impatient to move on.

The expedition set off again on July 15. Two men were still ailing but not enough to keep them from hiking along the bank. The journals noted a variety of things, both important and trifling. Mosquitoes and gnats made them miserable despite the mosquito nets they took pains to rig up each night. Chokecherries were getting ripe. When Drewyer wounded a deer, Lewis' dog, Scannon, swam into the

A modern photograph of the mountains near the Three Forks of the Missouri suggests what courage it took for the explorers to plunge deep into the trackless wilderness.

73

river, drowned it, and brought it back. The river had become so swift that the men seldom paddled the canoes any more but poled or towed them most of the time. And as the country became hillier, the buffalo disappeared. This meant renewed efforts at hunting other game, since it took four deer, or an elk and a deer, to replace the one buffalo that had kept the party adequately fed each day.

It was now very important that they meet the Shoshoni Indians, Sacagawea's tribe, to obtain horses and guides to take them across the mountains. But the Shoshonis were a backward and timid nation, persecuted by their warlike neighbors, the Blackfeet and Minnetarees. They lived almost entirely in the high mountains, using their horses, the only resource they possessed, to hunt and camp in the most inaccessible spots. They had learned to be wary of strangers.

The captains feared that the Shoshonis might hear the expedition's hunters shooting at game, and thinking them a war party, flee into the hills. To avoid this, Clark took four men and a supply of gifts and began traveling ahead of the main party in hopes of meeting the Shoshonis before they had a chance to be scared away. Lewis ordered the men to fly American flags on the canoes to show that they came in peace.

On July 22, Sacagawea began to recognize landmarks and told the captains that the place where the Mis-souri divided into three branches was not far ahead. Three days later, Clark's party reached the Three Forks of the Missouri and found the river they had followed so long split into three streams, each nearly ninety yards wide.

Although he was coming down with a high fever, Clark spent a couple of days exploring the area, looking unsuccessfully for Indian signs. On July 27 he rejoined Captain Lewis and the main party, which had meantime come up to the Forks. Lewis gave the ailing Clark a dose of Dr. Rush's bilious pills (his remedy for almost every complaint) and made him rest and bathe his feet, which were full of prickly pear thorns, in warm water.

To let Clark recover and to rest the men, who were all exhausted from laboring in the heat, Lewis determined to stay at the Three Forks for a few days. Sacagawea said that their camp was on the precise spot where her band of Shoshonis had been encamped five years earlier when the Minnetarees had attacked. The Shoshonis fled, but the Minnetarees pursued, killing and capturing a number of their enemies. Sacagawea, then about twelve years old, was among the prisoners taken.

"I cannot discover that she shews any immotion of sorrow in recollecting this event," Lewis wrote, "or of joy in being restored to her native country; if she has enough to eat and a few trinkets to wear I believe she would be perfectly content anywhere." But Lewis had never had much sym-

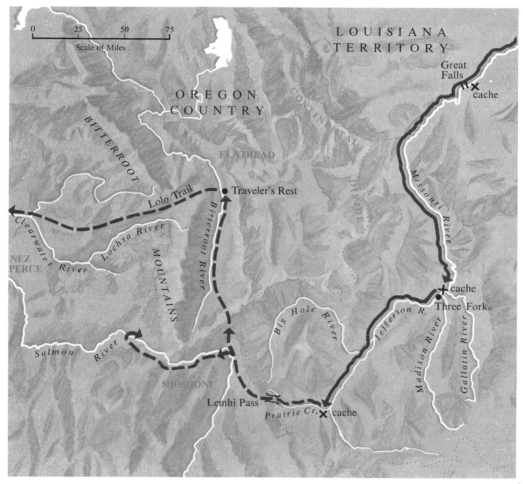

Leaving the Great Falls (top, right) on July 15, the expedition traveled up the Missouri past the Three Forks to the branching of Prairie Creek (lower right) and cached their canoes. Abandoning the Salmon River (lower left) as a route to the sea, they struck north and then west over the Lolo Trail. On October 7 they embarked on the Clearwater in fresh canoes.

pathy or understanding for Sacagawea; Clark, on the other hand, was to grow quite fond of her and her baby, Baptiste.

After a careful study of the Three Forks area the captains decided that none of the three nearly equal branches had a special right to be considered the Missouri's continuation. So they named the southwest branch the Jefferson River, the middle fork the Madison River for Secretary of State James Madison, and the southeast branch the Gallatin River for Secretary of the Treasury Albert Gallatin. All were clear, sparkling streams.

75

DOCTORING IN THE WILDERNESS

It seems amazing that Lewis and Clark's well-organized expedition set out to spend years in uncharted territory without taking along a doctor. At Wheeling, West Virginia, a young physician did, in fact, offer to join the party, but he failed to meet the deadline set by an impatient Lewis. Thanks to the men's remarkably sound constitutions, however, they managed to survive boils, dysentery, colic, frostbite, accidental wounds, bear and snake bites, dislocated limbs, influenza, starvation, and the drastic treatments administered by the captains. Major items in their medicine chest were jalap, a bitter purge made from the vine at top right, and Peruvian bark, or quinine (below, at left), with which Lewis cured a serious illness of Sacagawea's. Fortunately, he had inherited genuine medical ability from his mother, Lucy Meriwether Marks (above), who was famous for her skill in using herb remedies. Once, when he fell violently ill while separated from the main group and his chest of drugs, the captain daringly experimented by boiling twigs of chokecherry (far right) in water and drinking the nauseating black liquid. By nightfall he was free of pain and able to enjoy a refreshing and comfortable night's rest.

On July 30 they started up the Jefferson River, which they were convinced would lead them most directly into the mountains. The party was not in the best of condition. Clark, cured of his fever, now came down with what he called "the rageing fury of a tumer on my anckle" and was unable even to walk. Several men suffered from boils. Charbonneau had a bad leg. Sergeant Gass fell over a canoe and hurt his back. Drewyer, too, was disabled by a fall. Captain Lewis became ill with dysentery. Private Joseph Whitehouse's leg was badly bruised when his canoe overturned and the heavy dugout passed over him.

To add to their troubles, George Shannon, the youngest of the party, had gotten lost—something he rather frequently did. The previous summer he had been lost for sixteen days and kept himself alive by eating wild grapes. This time, the party was to spend three days searching for young Shannon before he returned to camp on his own, exhausted but unhurt.

The river became more rapid each day. The men struggled on, poling the canoes or wading and dragging them. At times they had to grasp the bushes on the banks to pull themselves against the swift current; in places they dragged the heavy craft over sand bars. Their feet, made tender by constant soaking, were badly bruised by the sharp stones.

On August 8 Sacagawea recognized a rock formation in the shape of a beaver's head. Not far away, she told the captains, her people used to cross the mountains in summer to a river that flowed to the west. This meant the Shoshonis must be somewhere nearby. There had already been many signs of Indians—smoke, trails by the river, a fresh moccasin print—but the explorers had not yet seen a person. It was vital that they cross the mountains before the fall snows, and they could not hope to find a route unaided. The next day, Lewis struck out overland with Drewyer, John Shields, and Hugh McNeal. He was determined not to return until he had met Indians.

The illustrator of the 1812 Gass Journal *depicted one of many occasions when the party's canoes capsized in mountain torrents. His well-dressed men in their neatly planked boat are far from the reality of dirty, bearded men in buckskins, struggling to right their awkward, heavy dugouts.*

After Lewis' party had ascended the valley of the Jefferson for a day, the river divided into two branches of about equal size, both impassable for canoes. At the fork Lewis left a note advising Clark to wait there until he returned. Lewis was following a trail left by Indian horses, and now it led up the westernmost of the branches, a stream known today as Prairie Creek.

The next morning they pushed on, walking abreast some distance apart, with Drewyer and Shields posted to right and left and Lewis and McNeal in the center. Suddenly, an Indian appeared on horseback, coming toward them over the plain. Through his telescope Lewis could see that he belonged to no nation they had met before, and he was certain the stranger was a Shoshoni.

Both Lewis and the Indian stopped when they were still about a mile apart. The captain brought out a blanket. Holding it by two corners, he tossed it into the air, and letting it unfold, pulled it down to earth. Repeating this signal three times was a universal sign of peace among Missouri River and Rocky Mountain Indians.

But while Lewis was showing his friendly intentions, Drewyer and Shields kept walking ahead. They were too far away to hear Lewis call, and Lewis was afraid to make any signals for fear of alarming the Shoshoni. It was an agonizing situation. All he could do was to leave his gun with McNeal and walk forward himself, holding up some trinkets as gifts.

An 1809 engraving of a Shoshoni chief, from an unauthorized book about the expedition, lacks the drama of Lewis' word portrait of Cameahwait "with his ferce eyes and lank jaw grown meager for the want of food." In his journal the captain drew the stone peace pipe (below), with its bowl set in the same line as the stem, which he smoked with the Shoshonis. The ceremony sealed a friendship that was to ensure the mission's success.

. . . [the Indian] remained in the same stedfast poisture untill I arrived in about 200 paces of him when he turn his ho[r]se about and began to move off slowly from me; I now called to him in as loud a voice as I could command repeating the word *tab-ba-bone*, which in their language signifyes *white-man*. But lo[o]king over his sholder he still kept his eye on Drewyer and Sheilds who wer still advancing. . . .

Obviously, the Indian was growing suspicious of the party's intentions.

In her lifetime, nobody paid much attention to the Shoshoni girl who traveled thousands of miles with the expedition, carrying her baby. By 1910, when this statue was put up, Sacagawea was an American heroine.

Although the captain succeeded in halting Drewyer with his signals, Shields kept plodding ahead. At last the Indian, plainly fearing a trap, turned his horse, jumped a creek, and vanished into some willows.

Disappointed, and furious with Shields for ruining their chance to meet the Shoshonis, Lewis decided not to risk alarming the tribe. Instead of following closely on the Indian's trail, he had the men build a fire and they breakfasted. In case any Indians should return, he put up a pole with some small gifts on it to show their peaceful intentions. Later, with Mc-Neal carrying a United States flag on a stick, they took up the trail of the Shoshoni horseman.

The next day, following the course of dwindling Prairie Creek, they at last came to its source, a spring they believed to be "the most distant fountain of the waters of the Mighty Missouri in surch of which we have spent so many toilsome days and wristless nights." A little earlier, Lewis recorded, McNeal "had exultingly stood with a foot on each side of this little rivulet and thanked his god that he had lived to bestride the mighty & heretofore deemed endless Missouri." Unaware that the true source of the Missouri is the easternmost of the two forks, not the one they had taken, they celebrated the achievement with an icy drink from the spring and went on.

Ahead a moderate rise led to a gap in the range of mountains. They followed the Indian trail up and through the pass and down the other side to "a handsome bold running Creek of cold Clear water. here I first tasted the water of the great Columbia river," wrote Lewis. He realized that, since the stream was flowing westward, they had crossed the Continental Divide. They had, in fact, come over what is now called Lemhi Pass, on the border formed by the Divide between Montana and Idaho, and were quenching their thirst in the Lemhi River, whose waters eventually reach the Columbia River. Since the Divide was the western limit of the Louisiana Territory, this also meant that they had left the United States and entered the disputed Oregon country.

The next day, August 13, they saw Indians again, this time two women and a man. The women fled instantly but the man let them approach to within one hundred yards before retreating. A mile farther on, however, they unexpectedly came upon three women in a ravine. A young woman dashed away to hide among the rocks, but an elderly woman and a twelve-year-old girl, seeing no opportunity to escape, bowed their heads as though to receive a deathblow.

Lewis took the woman's hand and raised her to her feet, repeating "tab-ba-bone" and pulling up his sleeve to prove that he really was white. His face and hands were sunburned as dark as their own. The explorers pulled some gifts out of their packs—beads, awls for sewing moccasins, mirrors, and face paint—which were eagerly accepted. The young woman who had fled was called back, and Lewis painted the cheeks of all three with vermilion, which Sacagawea had told him her people used as a symbol of peace. Then they all headed for the Shoshoni camp.

On the way they were intercepted by sixty mounted warriors, armed with bows and arrows and a few primitive muskets. Lewis at once laid down his gun and went forward with his flag, while the women explained what had happened and showed their presents. Lewis recorded the meeting:

These men then advanced and embraced me very affectionately in their way which is by puting their left arm over you[r] wright sholder clasping your back, while they apply their left cheek to yours and frequently vociforate the word âh-hí-e, âh-hí-e that is, I am much pleased, I am much rejoiced. bothe parties now advanced and we wer all carresed and besmeared with their grease and paint till I was heartily tired of the national hug.

In the Shoshoni camp, Lewis sat down with Cameahwait, their chief, for the parley on which so much depended. Now Drewyer proved his ability as an interpreter by using the sign language in which he was skilled to make the chief understand that Lewis' party came as friends. Before smoking the pipe of peace, the chief and all his warriors took off their moccasins and indicated that Lewis and his men should do the same. Cameahwait explained that this was to show how seriously they took this ceremony

Like all Indian tribes, the Shoshonis had many rituals and ceremonies involving medicine men, whom the captains called jugglers. A later medicine man used the staff at left, in the form of a crane; the decorated deer's-head cap at right was worn for a hunting dance.

of friendship, since it implied that if they broke their obligation, they would go barefoot.

As they smoked the pipe in turn, the women and children clustered around to stare at the first white men they had ever seen. Once the ceremonies were over, Lewis made further friends by distributing the rèst of his gifts among the onlookers. In return, the Shoshonis offered their visitors food, and Lewis' party, which had gone hungry for twenty-four hours, thankfully accepted the cakes made of dried berries, all the starving Indians had to eat.

That night there was a celebration with dancing lasting nearly all night, but Lewis went to bed at midnight. A friendly Indian had presented him with a piece of freshly roasted salmon, which proved they were close to the Pacific. Enough horses were tethered around the camp for Lewis to feel sure they could purchase as many as they needed. Profoundly relieved and ut-

Perpetually short of food and fearful of attack by more warlike tribes, the Shoshonis were constantly shifting camp. This sketch of burdened Indians moving into the hills, with dogs carrying baggage on crossed poles called travois, was made by Alfred Jacob Miller in 1837.

terly exhausted, the captain slept too soundly to hear more than an occasional yell from the Shoshoni entertainment in his honor.

After resting a day to give Clark and his party time to come up to the forks of the Jefferson, Lewis and his men set off to meet them on August 15, accompanied by Cameahwait and a small band of Shoshonis. As they traveled, several of the Indians began to grow fearful that the strangers were decoying them into a trap. Lewis sent Drewyer out to hunt, hoping to calm them down with the present of some food. But Drewyer came back empty-handed.

The next morning, however, Drewyer shot a deer. All the Indians instantly joined in a mad dash to the spot where the hunter was cutting up his prize. Once there, they fell upon the parts Drewyer was discarding "like a parcel of famished dogs each seizing and tearing away a part of the intestens." It was the first meat the Sho-

Charles M. Russell selected the expedition's encounter with the Flatheads, a minor incident in the crossing of the Rockies, because he wanted a Montana setting for a painting that now dominates one wall of Montana's House of Representatives. The warm Indian welcome better befits their earlier, decisive meeting with the Shoshonis. A guide (right) interprets for the captains, whose horses York holds, while Sacagawea sits nearby.

shonis had seen for days, and Lewis was happy to share it with them.

Filling their stomachs with the white men's kill made the Shoshonis somewhat more confident. Lewis now began to fear that Clark might not have had time to come up to the forks. If the white men were not at the rendezvous as Lewis had promised, the Indians would take fright all over

again and the whole mission might be ruined.

Seeing from some distance away that there was no sign of Clark's party at the forks, Lewis resorted to deception. He sent Drewyer forward to pick up his own note to Clark from the pole where he had left it six days earlier. Then he reassured Cameahwait by telling him that this was a note from his "brother Chief" informing him that Clark was coming slowly up the river. To prove his good faith, the captain suggested that Cameahwait send an escort with Drewyer to meet Clark. Lewis, Shields, and McNeal would stay behind with the main band of Shoshonis.

The chief assented, and Drewyer was ordered to set out at sunrise with

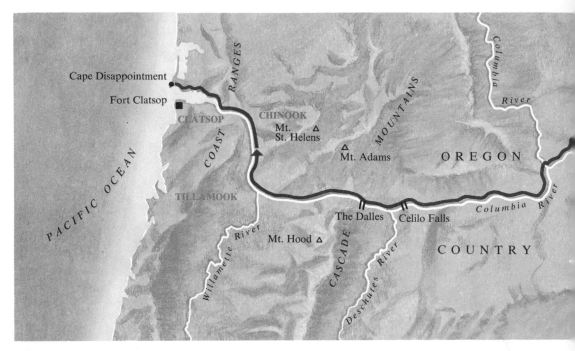

Trusting their horses to the Nez Percés, the party traveled the Clearwater (right) to its joining with the Snake, then took the Snake to the Columbia. Navigating the turbulent Great Falls (Celilo Falls) and The Dalles without mishap, they reached the Pacific at Cape Disappointment (left).

a hasty note from Lewis to Clark. Lewis tried to cheer up the nervous Cameahwait, most of whose warriors hid themselves in the bushes, convinced that there would be an enemy attack. With the chief close beside him, Lewis rigged his mosquito net and lay down, as worried as any of his hosts. What had happened to delay Clark and his party?

I slept but little as might be well expected, my mind dwelling on the state of the expedition which I have ever held in equal estimation with my own existence, and the fait of which appeared at this moment to depend . . . upon the caprice of a few savages who are ever as fickle as the wind.

Early the next day, August 17, Drewyer and his guides met the canoe party struggling up the river about

two miles below the forks where Lewis was waiting. Sacagawea, walking ahead with her husband and Clark, was the first to see them approaching. She began to dance with delight and make signs to Clark by sucking her fingers, which in sign language meant that these were her own people, who had nursed her as a baby. It was a joyous meeting, and the Shoshonis sang aloud as they escorted Clark and his party up to Lewis' camp.

At the forks of the river some amazing scenes took place. Sacagawea

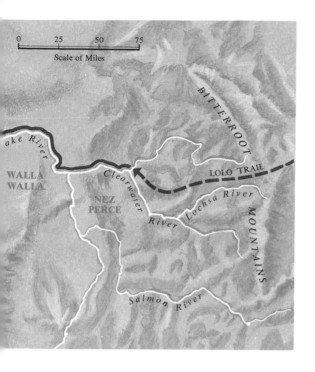

and one of the Shoshoni squaws with the party recognized and embraced each other with much emotion. Friends from childhood, they had both been taken prisoner by the Minnetarees and had shared captivity until the friend had escaped and found her way home. Neither had ever expected to see the other again.

Once Clark had been welcomed by Lewis, Cameahwait led him to a seat of honor and tied pearly shells in his red hair. When the captains began their council with the leading Shoshonis, an even more astonishing meeting occurred. Sacagawea, called in to interpret, had just sat down and was beginning to translate the first words when she suddenly recognized Cameahwait as her brother. Running over, she threw her arms around him and wept. Even after she had resumed interpreting, she was so moved that she broke into tears from time to time.

The council was a success. The Shoshonis desperately needed the white men's guns to kill game and keep off their enemies, and Cameahwait was willing to help the expedition by selling them horses. The captains agreed that Clark should reconnoiter Lemhi River as a possible canoe route to the Pacific. Lewis would meanwhile organize the transport of their supplies as far as the Shoshoni village, forty miles away.

On August 18 Clark set out with eleven men, while Lewis and the main party began repacking provisions and baggage into bundles suitable for carrying on horseback. What they could not take they cached, and the empty canoes were hidden by filling them with rocks and sinking them in a pond.

August 18 was also Lewis' thirty-first birthday, which he celebrated by catching some trout and reflecting solemnly in his journal that:

I had in all human probability now existed about half the period which I am to remain in this . . . world . . . that I had as yet done but little, very little, indeed, to further the hapiness of the human race or to advance the information of the succeeding generation . . . and resolved in future . . . to live for *mankind*, as I have heretofore lived *for myself.*

The captains had already asked Cameahwait about the topography of the area. By drawing lines on the ground to represent rivers and heaping up sand for mountains, the chief explained that the Lemhi River, on which his village stood, flowed into a large stream (the Salmon River) about eighteen miles away. But in passing between the mountains, Cameahwait said, the Salmon River was so hemmed in by cliffs that there was no shore to walk on. Furthermore, the mountains there were so high that neither man nor horse could cross them.

Up ahead, Clark was finding this out for himself. Led by an old Indian guide, Clark and his party spent four days confirming what Cameahwait had told them. Struggling along the Salmon River, the captain became convinced that it would be impossible

The forbidding range of the Bitterroots, which Patrick Gass called "the most terrible mountains I ever beheld," is photographed from the Lolo Trail, the route the famished explorers followed through the maze of snow-covered ridges, across passes six thousand feet high.

to take canoes through the turbulent, rock-filled water. They would have to rely on horses, but the mountains that edged the Salmon were too precipitous to cross. The guide then told Clark of a difficult trail that led a long distance to the north and then turned west over the mountains to another river that flowed westward. This was the route used by the Nez Percé Indians, who lived farther to the west, when they crossed the mountains to hunt buffalo on the plains.

When Clark returned to the Shoshoni village on August 29, Lewis and the main party were waiting for him. Despite their best trading, the captains could obtain only twenty-nine horses, not quite one for each member of the party. However, Clark's Shoshoni guide and his son agreed to be their escorts over the Nez Percé trail. Next day they set out after saying good-by to the friendly Shoshonis, who had delayed their annual hunting trip to the buffalo plains in order to bid them farewell. The expedition would never see them again.

Much nonsense has been written about Sacagawea and about how she guided Lewis and Clark to the Pacific. Actually, the only place where she recognized any landmarks during the trip was in the region near her birthplace. She of course helped as an interpreter with her own people, the Shoshonis. Nevertheless, the presence of a woman was instant proof to any Indian tribe Lewis and Clark met that their expedition was not a war party and had only peaceful intentions. This alone was enough to make her a valued member of the expedition.

Their trail now led north through the Bitterroot Mountains, along hillsides so steep that their horses were constantly falling. The men were too busy cutting a trail through the thick brush to have time to hunt. The weather was miserable: rain, snow, and sleet. At night they went to bed weary, hungry, and cold.

On September 4 they came down into a wide valley. Here they were met with great friendliness by a band of Flathead Indians (who, despite their name, have well-formed heads). It proved to be a fortunate meeting, for the Indians shared their food—berries and roots—with the expedition and sold them fresh horses.

The party continued north along the Bitterroot River, a little east of the present Montana-Idaho boundary. A week after their meeting with the Flatheads they stopped for a day on a creek, which they named Traveler's Rest. There the hunters stocked up on food before the party attempted the worst part of the trail, where their guides warned them no game could be found.

Then they turned west and for ten miserable days followed the difficult Lolo Trail over the Bitterroot Mountains. Snow lay on the ground, already strewn with fallen timber; several horses slipped and were hurt by rolling down steep slopes. At first they managed to shoot a few pheasant.

When their food gave out, they killed and ate first one colt, then a second and a third, "which we all Suped hartily on and thought it fine meat."

By September 18 the last colt was gone, and the expedition's supplies were reduced to "a skant proportion of portable soupe [a kind of instant broth that Lewis had purchased in Philadelphia] . . . a little bears oil and about 20 lbs. of candles." In desperation, Clark went ahead with six men to try to kill some game, while the rest of the party struggled on, growing weaker each day in body and in spirit.

On September 20 Clark's party came down into more level country, where there was an Indian village. Its inhabitants were Nez Percés. Though frightened at first, the Indians were friendly and offered the explorers dried salmon and pounded camass root, which promptly made the white men very sick. The Nez Percé chief, Twisted Hair, drew a map for Clark on a white elk skin. They were on the Clearwater River, and the Columbia was seven days' journey away.

On September 22 Lewis' exhausted party arrived, and like Clark's, instantly fell ill from the diet of fish and roots. Lewis himself took nearly two weeks to recover.

Meanwhile, Clark set the men, as they grew able, to work on making canoes. By October 6 they had completed four large dugouts and one small one. Their thirty-eight horses were branded and turned over to some of Twisted Hair's relations, who promised to take care of them. Twisted Hair himself and a lesser chief named Tetoharsky volunteered to guide them to the Columbia, and on October 7 they set off down the Clearwater. A day later their Shoshoni guides, intimidated by the Nez Percés now in the party, vanished.

On October 10 the expedition rode the waters of the Clearwater into a larger river (the Snake), which came up from the south, and at the joining swung to the northwest. At the forks the expedition crossed from the future state of Idaho into that of Washington. And on October 16 they passed from the Snake River into the Columbia. There was still a good distance to travel, but the end was now in sight.

The party camped at the confluence of the rivers and was soon joined by two hundred Indians, singing and beating drums, who had come from a village close by. Still chanting, they formed a semicircle while their chief smoked a ceremonial pipe with the captains and their Nez Percé guides. Indicating by signs that they wanted to be friends, the captains passed out medals and what gifts they could spare. The supply of trading goods and presents was rapidly dwindling.

As the canoes bobbed on the strong current above The Dalles of the Columbia, Clark noted "a mountain bearing S.W. conocal form Covered with Snow." In this 1954 photograph the cone of Mount Hood rises above a Columbia still swirling between the "black rugid rocks" Clark observed in 1805.

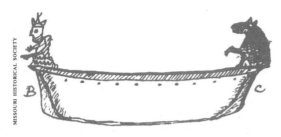

Admiring the canoes of the Columbia River tribes, "built of white cedar or Pine verry light wide in the middle and tapers at each end . . . with heads of animals carved on the bow," Clark sketched one in his diary.

Like all the Indians living on the great Columbia River and its tributaries, these people, the Sokulks, depended on the salmon that came up the river in incredible numbers. But at that season the salmon had stopped running and the river was filled with dead and dying fish. Clark recorded that:

those which was offerd to us we had every reason to believe was taken up on the shore dead [so] we thought proper not to purchase any, we purchased forty dogs [to eat] for which we gave articles of little value, such as beeds, bells & thimbles.

From the moment they had embarked on the Clearwater, the icy, swift-flowing water had been full of eddies and turbulent rapids. Several times, canoes had capsized or been crushed against the rocks, thereby losing the party some valuable stores. Now the Columbia began hurtling through a long series of canyons, and travel became increasingly perilous.

On October 22 they reached the rapids above the Great Falls of the Columbia, known afterward as Celilo Falls. Here they were obliged to portage their canoes and stores separately and to lower the canoes past the worst falls on ropes made of elk skin.

Reconnoitering ahead two days later, Captain Clark found new difficulties. A couple of miles downstream was The Dalles of the Columbia:

a tremendious black rock Presented itself high and Steep appearing to choke up the river; . . . at this place the water of this great river is compressed into a chanel between two rocks not exceeding forty five yards wide and continues for a 1/4 of a mile when it again widens.

Clark saw at once that they could not hope to portage the heavy canoes over the difficult rock, but Cruzatte, their most experienced waterman, agreed with him that with good handling, the canoes could be taken through the racing, slashing water:

accordingly I deturmined to pass through this place notwithstanding the horrid appearance of this agitated gut swelling, boiling & whorling in every direction, which from the top of the rock did not appear as bad as when I was in it; however we passed Safe to the astonishment of all the Inds. . . .

Their dangerous progress was watched by local Indians standing on the rocks above. Once safely through, the Americans were entertained by another group of Indians, who lived below The Dalles. Clark observed that their principal food was dried and pounded fish, and he counted "107 stacks . . . in different places on those rocks which must have contained 10,000 lb of neet fish." The captains celebrated the occasion by holding peace talks between these Indians and their two Nez Percé guides, while the men danced to the music of Cruzatte's violin.

After The Dalles area was passed, Twisted Hair and Tetoharsky said good-by to the captains, explaining that they could be of no further service because they did not understand the language of the tribes down-river. They had bought horses from a nearby village, and after a parting smoke they set off for home.

The expedition had to spend two days repairing the canoes, but it was water-borne again on October 28. By November 2 they had passed the Cascade Mountains with their countless splashing waterfalls and were at last on tidewater, where the ebb and flow of the Pacific began to be felt.

On November 7 came the moment they had been awaiting. "Ocian in view! O! the joy!" Clark wrote in the notebook he kept open constantly on his knee. That night he recorded in his journal:

Great joy in camp we are in view of the Ocian, this great Pacific Octean which we been so long anxious to See. And the roreing or noise made by the waves braking on the rockey Shores (as I suppose) may be heard disti[n]ctly.

An 1829 child's textbook of "Interesting Events in the History of the United States" honored Lewis and Clark's extraordinary achievement in reaching the Pacific unharmed with this picture of the party marching in correct military attire to the very edge of the ocean.

CLARK 19th Novr 1805

Chinnoah River

Cape Disappointment

S 88° W 11 m

Point Adams
Round

S 41° W 7 m

S 41° E 6 point Mill

Point Distress

East to point Mill

6 Encamped from 16th to 25th Novr 18

Chinnook old Villa

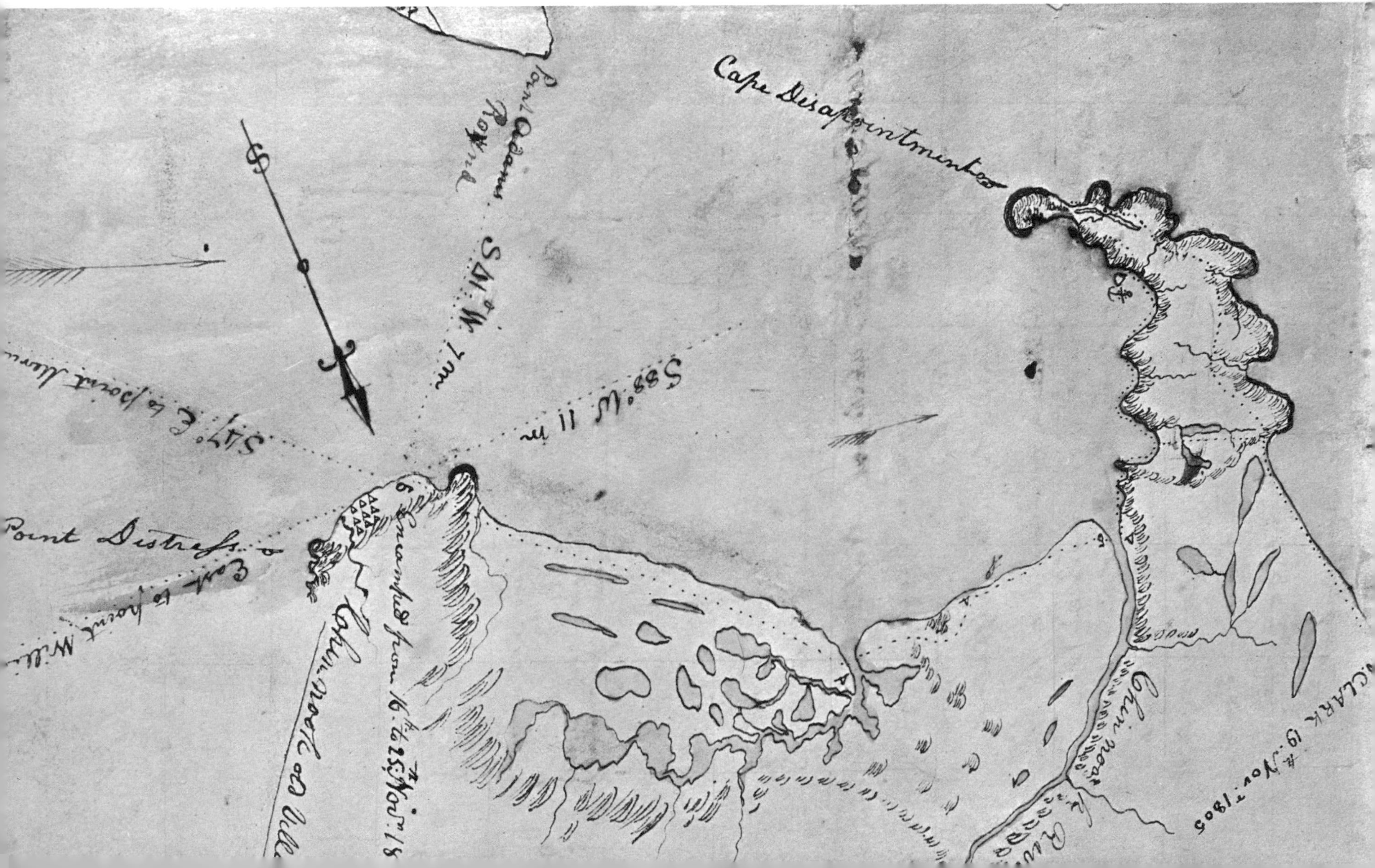

5

AN OREGON WINTER

Although they were so close to the Pacific, the captains and their weary men were far from reaching an end to their troubles. They were still a good number of miles from the mouth of the Columbia, but the river was now so wide—half a dozen miles or so—that some of the heaving and rolling of the ocean reached into the estuary. The clumsy canoes bobbed about like corks, and the men grew seasick.

On November 8, the day after Clark recounted his first sighting of the ocean, the expedition paddled another eight miles down-river but was finally forced by the rough water to go ashore on the north bank of the estuary. They found little refuge there, for the hills rose so steeply from the river that they could not leave the narrow beach. The water was too salty to drink, and they had to put their baggage on poles to keep it above the breaking waves. To complete their misery, the rain that had been falling all day—and for most of several previous days—continued all night.

The next day was even worse. It was still raining, and a brisk southerly wind began rolling huge ocean waves directly into the mouth of the estuary. Not only was the camping place flooded, but the high tide and waves started driftwood churning—and on the Columbia, driftwood meant dead trees as much as two hundred feet long and four to seven feet thick. Only desperate work saved the canoes from being crushed to pieces.

On the third day they moved a short distance, still in the rain, and made their camp in a gully where the drift logs had jammed into a solid pile just above water level. "The logs on which we lie is all on flote every high tide," wrote Clark miserably. All they had to eat was some dried pounded fish they had bought from the Indians

On Clark's map Cape Disappointment (top) curves across the Columbia estuary, which stretches from Point Adams (left) to Point Distress (right), where the party made its first dry camp beside a Chinook village.

OVERLEAF: *Unchanged since Clark described the "great swells brakeing against the rocks and Drift trees with great fury," Pacific rollers thunder on an Oregon beach under the gray sky of a present-day winter.*
RAY ATKESON

at the Great Falls. Joseph Fields went out to hunt meat for his famished comrades, but the hills were so steep and the undergrowth so dense that he could do nothing. The continuing downpour loosened stones on the steep hillsides, and they rolled down on the unhappy party.

On the fifth morning a gale of wind with lightning, thunder, hail, and violent rain endangered their camp. The expedition took advantage of a low tide that day to move about half a mile to a small brook where they were somewhat better protected. The next day, November 13, Captain Clark climbed the heights behind them with great effort because of their steepness and dense underbrush. When he reached the top, he could see nothing because of the heavy clouds. On his return three men, Colter, Willard, and Shannon, were sent down-river in a canoe to look for a safer campsite. The waves were again sending great logs of driftwood surging dangerously near their present spot.

The next morning five Indians arrived in a canoe and managed to land despite the constant rain and high waves. Shortly afterward, John Colter came striding back along the shore and he at once accused the Indians of having just robbed him of his fishing gear. Not until a gun was aimed at them would the Indians give up the stolen articles. Such thievery was to be a constant problem in Oregon.

Colter reported that he and his comrades had found a "butifull Sand beech" just around the point and that Willard and Shannon had gone ahead to spy out the land. That afternoon Lewis with a party of four set out to look for a sheltered bay at the mouth of the Columbia where, according to the Indians, the white sea captains usually anchored their trading vessels. Five men took Lewis' party by canoe as far as the beach Colter had found. They struggled back at dusk with their craft almost awash in the high waves.

At camp Clark made some unhappy observations about the condition of the expedition's supplies:

The rain &c. which has continued without a longer i[n]termition than 2 hours at a time for ten days past has distroyd the robes and rotted nearly one half of the fiew clothes the party has, perticularley the leather clothes. If we have cold weather before we can kill & Dress Skins for clothing the bulk of the party will Suffer . . .

Soon after parting from John Colter, Alexander Willard and George Shannon had met a band of about twenty Indians. The natives were so excessively friendly that the two white men grew suspicious. But the Indians would not leave them, and Willard and Shannon feared they would be murdered during the night. After sitting up late around the campfire with their unwelcome guests, the two finally lay down with their rifles under their heads.

In the morning the guns were gone. When the Indians refused to return them, Shannon picked up a club. He was about to use it on a man he suspected, when another Indian began to load a musket and Shannon wisely put his weapon down. By signs Shannon warned the Indians that if they did not give up the stolen rifles, a party of white men would come down the river and kill every one of them. By the greatest of luck, Lewis and his party appeared just at that moment on their way to the ocean, and the terrified Indians gave up the guns to Willard and Shannon immediately.

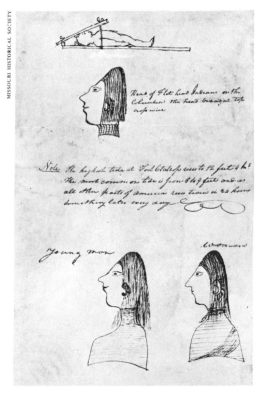

Clark's drawings show how the Chinook Indians flattened their infants' heads to a breadth of less than two inches by binding them between boards (top) for their first year of life. This produced the straight line from tip of nose to top of head that they prized in adult men and women (below).

The captains had little respect for the Indians of the lower Columbia. Clark grudgingly conceded that the women of the Chinooks, the chief nation of the area, had handsome faces. Otherwise, he wrote, they were "low and badly made with large legs & thighs which are generally Swelled from a Stopage of the circulation in the feet (which are Small) by maney strands of Beeds . . . drawn tight around the leg above the ankle." He could find nothing good to say about the appearance of the men: "The Men are low homely and badly made, Small crooked legs large feet, and all of both Sects have flattened heads." The Chinooks achieved these flattened heads by compressing the foreheads of their infants between two padded boards. It was not painful, nor did it apparently affect intelligence, but it left the shape of the head permanently altered.

Compared with most white men of the period, Lewis and Clark were tolerant of the Indians' odd physical appearance and customs. What annoyed them was the natives' habit of stealing everything in sight. The Indians were such skillful thieves that, even when closely watched, they often managed to make off with something.

However, there was one distinction that none of the party denied them: they were the finest boat handlers the white men had ever seen, and they could take their big, well-designed canoes over the roughest water with the greatest skill and ease.

NAVIGATORS OF THE NORTHWEST

Sir Francis Drake was the first European to glimpse the Oregon coastline, as he searched vainly for the Northwest Passage in 1579. Two centuries later, Britain's famous navigator Captain James Cook (above, far left) explored Nootka Sound on his way north to Alaska. Cook's official artist depicted a Nootka Indian house (left) in 1779, with its carved totems and rafters festooned with drying fish. Once Cook's returning sailors realized the fabulous value of the sea-otter furs they had purchased from the Nootkas for trifles, trading ships began flocking to the Pacific coast. In 1790 Captain Robert Gray made a fur-trading voyage there from Boston, and an eyewitness sketched him (above) superintending construction of a second ship, with his *Columbia* anchored nearby. Sailing southward in 1792, he passed British Captain George Vancouver (above, near left), who was sailing north to complete and expand Cook's survey work. The captains exchanged information about the coast, then sailed on—Gray to discover the Columbia River, Vancouver to circumnavigate the island now named in his honor. Their respective feats were to establish America's claim to the Oregon country and Britain's to British Columbia.

Dear Sir   Washington. U.S. of America. July 4. 1803.

In the journey which you are about to undertake for the discovery of the course and source of the Missouri, and of the most convenient water communication from thence to the Pacific ocean, your party being small, it is to be expected that you will encounter considerable dangers from the Indian inhabitants. should you escape those dangers and reach the Pacific ocean, you may find it imprudent to hazard a return the same way, and be forced to seek a passage round by sea, in such vessels as you may find on the Western coast. but you will be without money, without clothes, & other necessaries; as a sufficient supply cannot be carried with you from hence. your resource in that case can only be in the credit of the US. for which purpose I hereby authorise you to draw on the Secretaries of State, of the Treasury, of War & of the Navy of the US. according as you may find your draughts will be most negociable, for the purpose of obtaining money or necessaries for yourself & your men: and I solemnly pledge the faith of the United States that these draughts shall be paid punctually at the date they are made payable. I also ask of the Consuls, agents, merchants & citizens of any nation with which we have intercourse or amity, to furnish you with those supplies which your necessities may call for, assuring them of honorable and prompt retribution. and our own Consuls in foreign parts where you may happen to be, are hereby instructed & required to be aiding & assisting to you in whatsoever may be necessary for procuring your return back to the United States. And to give more entire satisfaction & confidence to those who may be disposed to aid you I Thomas Jefferson, President of the United States of America, have written this letter of general credit for you with my own hand, and signed it with my name.

Th. Jefferson

To
    Capt. Meriwether Lewis.

In case Lewis should need to return from the Pacific by ship, Jefferson personally wrote out this remarkable "letter of general credit." It authorized him to draw "on the Secretaries of State, of the Treasury, of War & of the Navy of the U.S. . . . for the purpose of obtaining money or necessaries for yourself & your men." Lewis carried this priceless letter to the Pacific and back but never needed to use it.

In defense of these Indians, it should be said that their decline in manners and morals seemed to have been hastened by the coming of the white man. Fur traders had brought them not only kettles, beads, and guns, but also disease, and treated them with brutal contempt.

While Lewis was gone, Clark managed during a brief lull in the wind to move camp a short distance downriver from the miserable spot where they had been living. Their new camp was on a sandy beach, and with no timber nearby, they were forced to break their usual rule of never taking anything that belonged to the Indians without paying a fair price for it. To build their huts, they helped themselves to boards from a nearby Chinook village, "deserted by the Inds & in full possession of the flees." (They had found every Indian village below the Great Falls of the Columbia, even those long deserted, to be infested with fleas.) From their new camp they had a wide view of the ocean, from Cape Disappointment on the north side of the Columbia estuary to Point Adams on the south.

When Lewis returned to camp on November 17, Clark announced that anyone else who wanted to see the "main Ocian" should be ready to start early the next morning. Ten men "and my man York" went with him, traveling by land along the stream-cut beach that lay between their camp and Cape Disappointment. There they climbed a hill and tried to make out where the main channel of the Columbia entered the ocean, but the meeting of the river and the sea brought such crashing waves right across the broad estuary that it was impossible to decide where the deepest channel lay. In a sense, they were having the same trouble that had led John Meares, the British sea captain who explored the area in 1788, to name the headland Cape Disappointment. Meares, eagerly seeking the Great River of the West, believed he had failed to find it because he did not recognize that the bay concealed the mouth of the Columbia.

Clark's party camped on the shores of the Pacific itself, making their supper on pounded fish, some wild geese they had shot, and a flounder swept in by the waves. Clark noted: "Men appear much Satisfied with their trip beholding with estonishment the high waves dashing against the rocks & this emence Ocian."

The next day they explored, going north and then returning to the river without discovering anything important. They did meet small parties of Indians, who were always coming and going, and on their return to camp found Lewis entertaining many Chinooks, including two chiefs.

One of the Indians wore a magnificent sea-otter robe, which the captains tried to purchase. The owner would accept only blue beads—which the Indians of the Pacific Northwest treasured more than anything else. But although the captains had red and white beads left in their meager supply of trading goods, there was a serious shortage of blue beads. Most of the blue beads in the camp were in a belt that Sacagawea wore around her waist. Lewis and Clark offered her a "coate of Blue Cloth" in exchange, she willingly gave up the belt, and they were able to buy the otter robe after all.

Except for very brief periods, it rained continually. Clark, who was heartily sick of the autumn weather of the Pacific Northwest coast, struck a note of despair in his November 22 entry: "O! how horriable is the day waves brakeing with great violence against the Shore throwing the Water into our Camp &c. all wet and confind to our Shelters."

Hunting had been poor, and when on November 24 the hunters brought in only a single goose, the captains were forced to make some hard decisions about where the expedition would spend the winter. The Chinooks who lived nearby depended mainly on dried fish and roots for winter food, but they did not appear to have much to spare. In any case, the prices they asked were so high that the expedition's small store of trade goods could not possibly buy enough food to carry them through the winter. The captains still hoped to replenish their equipment and stores by purchasing goods from a trading ship, but they certainly could not count on such a source of supply.

They would have to depend on their guns for food. The Indians told them that they would find deer upriver, while elk were more numerous to the south, on the opposite shore of the Columbia. Elk were larger than deer and easier to kill, and their hides could more easily be made into clothing—which the party also desperately needed. There would be certain ad-

vantages to a move upriver, but by remaining near the ocean, their chances of sighting a trading ship were greatly increased. Only on the ocean, too, could they make salt, which they had been short of for a long time. The two commanding officers took their usual step of talking the matter over with the men, and Patrick Gass recorded that "most of them were of opinion, that it would be best . . . to go over to the south side of the river, and ascertain whether good hunting ground could be found there." On November 26 they moved to the south bank.

For a time they were almost as miserable as they had been on the north side of the river. The land was low and marshy, the rains continued, and although hunters went out every day, they came home empty-handed. The expedition had little else to eat

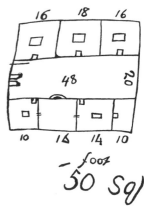

Clark's sketch plan for Fort Clatsop, reproduced above, at right, gives the dimensions of its seven small rooms, built in a fifty-foot square that was entered by a gate in the southern stockade. In an engraving from Gass' Journal *(above, left) the men raise the first posts of the line of cramped sheds. At right, in a modern reconstruction, Fort Clatsop once again flies the American flag on the site where the expedition spent the dreary winter of 1805–06.*

but the pounded fish they had bought at the falls one month earlier. By December 2 Clark was observing that this was causing so much sickness among the men that a change of diet was absolutely necessary. This complaint was being taken care of that very day, for Joseph Fields shot an elk six miles from the camp, and several men set off in a canoe to bring it in. The sun shone briefly as they returned next day in triumph with the carcass. It was the first elk they had killed west of the Rockies, and it provided a feast that raised everyone's spirits.

With several men Lewis spent nearly a week exploring the boggy country and finally selected a site for a winter camp three miles up a small stream he named Netul River—today it is Lewis and Clark River—flowing into the Columbia. There, on a slight rise well above high tide, amid a grove of tall firs, the main party began building cabins on December 8. Clark was especially happy to leave the mouth of the Columbia:

The sea which is imedeately in front roars like a repeeted roling thunder and have rored in that way ever since our arrival in its borders which is now 24 days since we arrived in sight of the Great Western Ocian, I cant say Pasific as since I have seen it, it has been the reverse.

The men worked in the rain to to build their cabins. The bad weather was affecting them; a number were ill, and several had boils. Their elk meat spoiled in the humid air, although they smoked it over a constant small fire. The pounded fish, on which they still depended in emergencies, was becoming moldy. The one consolation was that they had plenty of fine timber

The coastal Indians' custom of burying their dead in canoes, which the captains observed in 1806, was depicted by a British artist, Henry Warre, who visited the Columbia in 1845.

to build their fort. Gass, the ex-carpenter, noted how easily it split into boards "10 feet long and 2 broad, not more than an inch and a half thick."

By Christmas Day the camp was almost complete and all the party were snugly fixed in their huts. The captains handed out tobacco to the men who used it, and gave a handkerchief each to the nonsmokers. But their attempts to have a merry Christmas fell a little flat, as Clark revealed:

We would have Spent this day the nativity of Christ in feasting, had we any thing either to raise our Sperits or even gratify our appetites, our Diner concisted of pore Elk, so much Spoiled that we eate it thro' mear necessity, Some Spoiled pounded fish and a fiew roots.

The camp was completed on December 30, 1805, and named Fort Clatsop after the friendly Indians who were their neighbors. Unlike Fort Mandan, it was square. Four small cabins set in a row fifty feet long faced another row of three cabins twenty feet away. Palisades of sharpened posts connected the ends of the two rows and on the southern side there was a pair of gates, in front of which a sentry regularly stood guard.

By now the expedition's salt supply had long been exhausted, and the men craved something to mask the

106

taste of rotten meat and fish. Five men, equipped with "5 of the largest Kittles" were sent to the ocean to find a good place to make salt. This was done by boiling sea water over a slow fire until the water evaporated and the dry salt encrusting the kettles could be scraped into a keg. Early in January the salt-makers sent back a gallon of fine white salt and the welcome tidings that they could produce more at the rate of almost a gallon a day.

The stranding of a whale on the coast caused considerable excitement, and on January 5 a party of men was ordered to be ready to start the next morning in the hope of obtaining some blubber. Sacagawea, who had always done everything asked of her without complaint, now insisted that she be permitted to go. She had traveled a long way to see the great waters, she said, and now, with a huge fish also to be seen, she thought it would be very unfair to be left behind. She got her way, and she and her baby were included in the party.

When they reached the whale, they found that the Indians had reduced it to a vast skeleton. After much haggling, Captain Clark was able to buy three hundred pounds of blubber and a few gallons of whale oil from the Tillamook Indians who had cut up the huge beast. "Small as this stock is," he wrote, "I prise it highly . . . and think [God] much more kind to us than he was to jonah, having Sent this Monster to be Swallowed by us in Sted of Swallowing of us as jonah's did."

Life at Fort Clatsop settled into a rain-soaked routine. Although the supply of game was adequate, the animals at that time of year were thin and their meat was poor. If it had not been for Drewyer, the party would have gone very hungry. On one day alone he brought in seven elk, and Clark noted in his journal that none of their other hunters had his knowledge or skill in killing these beasts, their principal source of food. The salt-makers on the coast fifteen miles to the southwest kept their kettles boiling night

Clark's daily notes in a weather diary for January, 1806, vary little from the same depressing theme: "Sun visible for a fiew minits," or "rained verry hard last night."

and day, but the supply of salt grew very slowly. The men tanned elk skins and made new clothing and moccasins for the long trip back. A count made on March 12 showed 358 pairs of moccasins and many tanned elk skins on hand. During the long rainy days and evenings Lewis and Clark worked over their notes on plants, animals, weather, Indians, geography, and everything else they had observed since leaving Fort Mandan, organizing the mountain of information and putting it into readable form.

They were still hoping to make contact with a British or American trading ship. Painstakingly, both captains questioned the Indians about the traders who regularly visited them, how long they stayed, and when they

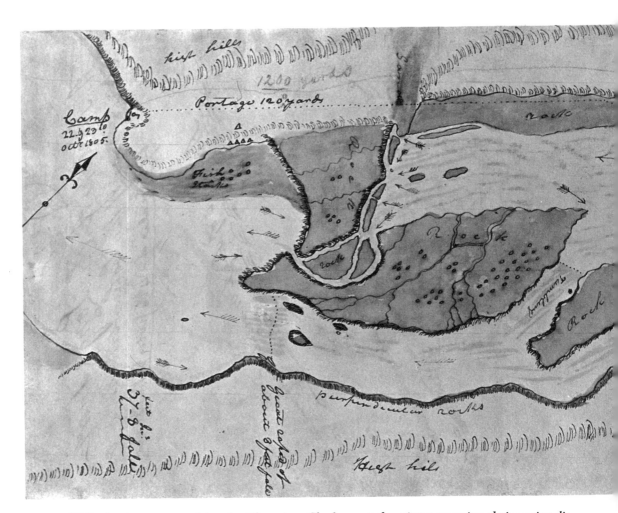

While Lewis wrote out his scientific notes, Clark spent the winter mapping their major discoveries. Above, a dotted line (top) marks the portage past the Great Falls of the Columbia, raging below the islands at center. The canoes shot a narrow channel above the main island.

were expected to return. They had built their fort close to the ocean chiefly because they would thereby be able to keep track of any visiting vessels. President Jefferson's original instructions called for two of the expedition's members to return by sea from the west coast, if it were possible. More important still, they badly needed to acquire fresh stocks of trad-ing goods before the rest of the party made the long return trip by land. One of the great mysteries of the expedition is why Jefferson did not send a ship to the mouth of the Columbia to meet them. One historian has suggested that the President was not inclined to risk offending Spain by dispatching a ship to the Pacific coast. Ironically, in fact, an American trading vessel was in the area all the time.

A Boston brig named the *Lydia* had arrived on the northwest coast in the spring of 1805, to trade and buy furs. After spending the summer farther to the north, she re-entered the mouth of the Columbia that November, close to the time when Lewis and Clark were vainly seeking traders in the area of Cape Disappointment. All through that winter the *Lydia* plied along the coast, but the Indians apparently failed to tell her captain that his fellow Americans were encamped at Fort Clatsop—until the entire expedition had left on the return journey.

The rainy winter turned into a rainy spring, and the captains decided to leave Fort Clatsop on or before April 1. As it was, they had barely enough supplies to get them to their cache on the forks of the Jefferson River. Moreover, the elk on which they chiefly depended for food had moved inland toward the mountains.

They purchased one canoe for Lewis' dress uniform coat and half a twist of tobacco, but to the lower Columbia Indians a canoe was a man's most valuable possession, worth as

AMERICAN PHILOSOPHICAL SOCIETY, PHILADELPHIA

One of Clark's finest drawings is this salmon trout, which occupies a whole page of his diary for March, 1806. Since the fish and its close relative, the salmon, were as vital to the Columbia River Indians as the buffalo was to those along the Missouri, Clark included a full description, which he copied (as he often did when pressed for time) from Lewis.

much as or even more than a wife. The captains could not buy another. In the end, they simply took a second canoe, telling themselves that it was a fair exchange for some elk the Clatsops had stolen during the winter.

The captain's last task was to fill in the date of their departure on several records of their visit. These they left with various Indians, to be turned over to any visiting white traders. Shortly afterward, one of these papers was actually given to the captain of the *Lydia*, who carried the news of their achievements to Canton in China. From there a copy of the message finally reached Philadelphia, nearly a year after the members of the expedition had returned to civilization.

Presenting Fort Clatsop, their home for three months, to Comowool, the most helpful of the Clatsop chiefs, the explorers started home in a brief spell of sunshine on March 23, 1806.

As they made their way up the Columbia River, they passed tribe after tribe of Indians. They had met many of the same Indians going down-river the previous year, and most were friendly and hospitable. The captains found them quite ready to sell roots, fish, or other food, but their prices were often too high for the expedition.

On April 1 they met Indians who said they lived at the rapids near the Great Falls. Their store of pounded salmon had given out, and because they did not expect that season's salmon run to begin until early May, they had come down hoping to find food in the valley. The news was a blow to the captains. They had planned to buy enough of the dried, pounded fish at the rapids to carry them through to the Nez Percé country, for game would be scarce above the Great Falls.

To solve the problem, the expedition camped. Parties of hunters went out to shoot elk and deer while the men in camp set up scaffolds for jerking the meat they brought back.

While Lewis supervised the camp, Clark and a small party of men spent two days exploring the great river that emptied into the Columbia some 140 miles from the ocean. The Indians called it the Multnomah; it has since been rechristened the Willamette.

With his usual resourcefulness, Clark also managed to coax an unfriendly Indian family into giving him some food by doing a little "magic." First, he made their campfire crackle and change color by throwing in some

This compass, on a chain that could attach it to a vest or belt, accompanied Clark on the trip and is almost certainly the one he used to awe the Indians with his "magic."

"port fire match"—a kind of slow-burning artillery fuze. Then he pulled out his pocket compass, and using the magnet in the top of his portable inkstand, "turned the needle of the compas about very briskly; which astonished and alarmed these nativs." Imploring him to "take out the bad fire," they piled bundles of roots at his feet, and Clark stopped whirling the needle just as the port fire burned out and the flames returned to normal. The frightened Indians "took shelter in their beads [beds]," but when Clark paid them a fair price for their roots, they were "somewhat passified."

Four days later, they were on their way again, with enough dried meat to take them to the Nez Percé villages. On April 9 the party reached the end of tidewater, and the next day the familiar, painful fight against rapids began; most of the first day they had to use a towrope. As they progressed,

At the Great Falls, later called Celilo Falls, the captains saw many Indians standing on wooden platforms to scoop salmon out of the Columbia River with nets. The catch was so great that thousands of pounds of fish were stacked to dry on nearby rocks. Through the generations the Indians went on fishing from exactly the same spots until water backed up by The Dalles Dam down-river inundated the falls in 1957, soon after this photograph was taken.

however, they were able to buy horses from Indians along the way, and they either cut up their canoes for fuel or sold them, one after another. By the time they reached the Great Falls of the Columbia, the uppermost of the obstacles, only two small canoes remained to be portaged around the falls. The rest of their baggage was on nine of the horses they had obtained; a tenth carried a sick man. William Bratton had been suffering all winter from mysterious pains in his back and was no longer able to walk.

They were happy to get away from the rapids. The Indians there had been surly and so thievish that they sometimes almost stole articles out of the men's hands. One band, the Wahclellahs, had even tried to steal Lewis' dog, Scannon. Fortunately, an Indian who spoke Clatsop told Lewis of the theft. Three men were sent to the Indian village at once and saved Scannon from being made into stew.

So many things were stolen that when Lewis detected one man attempting to make off with an iron fitting for a canoe, he "gave him several severe blows and mad[e] the men kick him out of camp." It was apparently the first time either Lewis or Clark had become so exasperated as to raise a hand against an Indian.

By April 24, after days of bickering with the Indians for a fair price, they were able to buy three more horses. Selling the two remaining canoes for a few strands of beads, they continued their journey on horseback over the stony, barren uplands that bordered the Columbia River.

A few days later, they were welcomed by the Walla Walla Indians whom they had met on the trip west. These hospitable people not only fed them and sold them ten dogs—the party was living pretty much on fresh dog and dried elk—but also gave them three horses and sold them two more. A day after the explorers had left, the helpful Walla Walla chief sent three young men riding after them to return a steel trap they had forgotten.

After following the Columbia River until it turned north, they cut directly across country to the east. As they neared Nez Percé territory, they were met by ten Nez Percé warriors led by their chief Weahkoonut, whom the party knew from the previous fall. He had heard they were on their way back and had come to greet them. Soon they were seeing Nez Percé homes and people. One of the first persons they met was Tetoharsky, the younger of the two chiefs who had guided the expedition safely past the Great Falls on its outward journey.

The next day, May 5, the Indians delivered to Clark a horse bearing Lewis' own brand. It was one of those they had turned over for safekeeping to the chief they called Twisted Hair. If the rest of their mounts were in equally good condition, the explorers could at least count on having enough horses to carry them over the Divide. Then only bad weather could stand in the way of their success.

6

RETURN TO CIVILIZATION

The captains were relieved to be once again among the friendly Nez Percés. However, the famished party had no more food left and the Indians had little but roots to spare. With their trading goods almost gone, the ingenious Americans cut off the buttons from their few remaining coats—no longer needed since the party was clad entirely in skins—and bartered them for something to eat. The captains' medical knowledge, however, proved much more profitable. Clark especially had gained a reputation as a healer during their previous visit, and now ailing Indians came flocking to the camp in large numbers, offering food in exchange for treatment.

Clark salved his conscience by noting:

in our present situation I think it pardonable to continue this deception for they will not give us any provisions without compensation in merchendize, and our stock is now reduced to a mear handfull. We take care to give them no article which can possibly injure them, and in maney cases can administer & give such medicine & sirgical aid as will effectually restore in simple cases &c.

Some of the cases they were to cure, however, were not so simple and amazed the captains as well as their admiring patients. One such was the wife of a chief, who had an abscess on her back that Clark believed beyond help. But, at the Indians' insistence, he opened the ugly infection and treated it. The woman began to recover at once, and the chief rewarded Clark with a horse—which the party at once killed and ate.

On May 8 they set out with a chief named Cut Nose—because of a nostril slit in battle—to find Twisted Hair and the horses that he had been tending for them since the previous autumn. But when they located Twisted Hair, the two chiefs began shouting at each other. It took the captains some time to separate the truth from the conflicting stories told by Twisted Hair and Cut Nose, but it appeared that Twisted Hair had permitted his young men to hunt with the expedition's horses. They had misused the animals until Cut Nose and another chief, Broken Arm, had stepped in and taken charge of the mounts. Thanks

Three decades after Lewis and Clark braved the challenge of the Rockies, Alfred Jacob Miller romantically contrasted the massive barrier of peaks with two minute horsemen (right).

115

to the captains' diplomacy, the two chiefs were reconciled, and most of the horses and saddles were recovered in good condition the next day.

A day later, May 10, they moved on some sixteen miles to the village of Broken Arm, the principal chief of the Nez Percés, which Lewis described:

The village of the broken arm consists of one house or Lodge only which is 150 feet in length built in the usual form of sticks mat and dry grass. it contains twenty-four fires and about double that number of families. . . .the noise of their women pounding roots reminds me of a nail factory.

Since several important chiefs had ridden there to see them, Lewis and Clark arranged a council to tell the Nez Percés about the United States government's desire to bring peace and trade to its red brothers. It was not easy to convey the message. One of the captains would say a few phrases, which Drewyer or Labiche would translate into French for Charbonneau, who would then translate them into Minnetaree for Sacagawea. She, in turn, would put them into Shoshoni, while a Shoshoni prisoner of the Nez Percés was able to make the final translation into Nez Percé. "the interpretation being tegious it occupied the greater part of the day," Clark wrote.

The council was a success, although the chiefs would not definitely commit themselves to sending men with the expedition to guide them across the mountains. Since there was no point in setting out until the snow

melted in the high passes, the captains decided to move camp several miles to the banks of the Clearwater River. Here the hunting was better, their horses had plenty of grazing, and there was the hope of netting fresh salmon once the fish started running. Their only real problem was the health of William Bratton, who, unable to sit up without great pain, was in no condition to journey over the Divide.

John Shields observed that he "had seen men in a similar situation

OLIN D. WHEELER, *The Trail of Lewis and Clark*, 1904, G. P. PUTNAM'S SONS

In 1901, the year of this photograph, Pe-tow-ya, a 110-year-old Indian woman, clearly recalled Lewis and Clark's 1806 visit and their miraculous cure of her sick father.

restored by violent sweats," and Bratton, as desperate for a cure as his captains, agreed to the heroic treatment.

Shields dug a pit four feet deep, lined it with rocks, and kindled a fire on top of them. When the rocks were hot enough, he removed the fire and rigged up a seat across the hole onto which Bratton, stripped naked, was lowered. Bratton then poured water onto the rocks to make as much steam as he could bear. After about twenty minutes the patient was "taken out and suddonly plunged in cold water twise and was then immediately returned to the sweat hole." Here he stewed for another forty-five minutes, drinking copious draughts of mint tea, before he was taken out, wrapped in blankets, and "suffered to cool gradually." Next day, a joyful Bratton was walking about almost free from pain.

The Nez Percés were still besieging Clark, "their favorite phisician," for medical aid. The near-miracle of Bratton's recovery was so remarkable that the captains decided to give the same treatment to one of the most hopeless Indian cases, a chief who had been paralyzed and unable to move hand or foot for three years. The chief's father volunteered to hold the helpless man upright in the hole and endured the steam bath along with his son. Next day, the chief was able to move his arms; a day later he could wash his face. After another steaming, he could move one of his legs, and in the next few days he amazed everyone by recovering the use of all his limbs.

Late in May Sacagawea's baby son, who had survived one hardship after another in his fifteen months of life, had bad teething troubles. His face swelled dangerously and he began to run a high fever, with an abscess behind his ear. In spite of poultices of wild onion and doses of "cream of tarter &c.," the little boy grew worse for several days, and the captains made several worried entries in their journals before he began to recover.

Game continued scarce and so did fish. "Patience, patience," Lewis wrote. Daily he watched the river for signs of floodwater from the melted snows of "that icy barier which seperates me from my friends and Country, from all which makes life esteemable."

Although the Nez Percés were friendly, they were reluctant to guide the Americans over the Rockies for fear of being attacked by the Blackfeet and Minnetarees, who tyrannized over the tribes to the east. Unwilling to wait any longer for guides to join them, the captains and their men set out on June 10 to find their own way over the Bitterroot Mountains. But once they got up into the high country, they found the snow still twelve or fifteen feet deep in many places and knew that they would never be able to follow the trail.

It was a bitter blow to have to turn back, "the first time . . . on this long tour that we have ever been compelled to retreat," wrote Lewis. Leaving

"Our camp is agreeably situated in . . . an extensive level and beautifull prarie," wrote Lewis on June 12, 1806. Weippe Prairie, Idaho, is pictured here as the explorers saw it, with the camass in flower, when "from the colour of its bloom at a short distance it resembles lakes of fine clear water." The camass, an edible bulb related to the lily family, was a mainstay of Indian life; it could be eaten boiled or pounded into cakes. John Collins, a drinking man, even managed to make root beer out of some camass that had gone sour.

Soldier-artist Gustavus Sohon, crossing the Bitterroots with a party of explorers in 1855, sketched men and horses struggling over the snowy trail that Lewis and Clark took in 1806.

most of their baggage piled on scaffolds above the snow, they returned to the camass flats of the valley once more. There they waited until they could persuade five Nez Percés to guide them over the mountains.

They followed almost exactly the trail they had taken the previous autumn, moving as fast as they dared, because there would be no grazing for their horses until they had crossed the perilous mountains. This time, however, it was easier. Although they often skirted precipices where a slip would have plunged a horse to its death, there were no accidents. Even the deepest snow was so firm that the horses' hoofs sank into it no more than two or three inches, and it covered many of the rocks and logs that had made traveling difficult before. Although food grew scarce, they did not have to kill and eat their horses as they had on their earlier crossing.

On June 29 they crossed the Lolo Pass and were over the Bitterroot Mountains. That night they stopped to camp by some hot springs, where they all bathed. Clark stayed in the hot water for ten minutes; Lewis, though sweating profusely, managed nineteen.

The next day they reached Traveler's Rest, the camp where they had prepared for the mountain crossing the autumn before. Game was now abundant for the first time in many weeks, and men and horses rested as the captains paid off their guides and planned the details of their next move.

After leaving the Great Falls of the Missouri on their way west, the explorers had swung in a giant U-shaped path. They had traveled south up the Missouri and the Jefferson, then cut west over Lemhi Pass, and finally turned north, following the Bitterroot River to Traveler's Rest.

For years after his return Clark worked at mapping the country through which the party ha
traveled. From his many sketch maps and daily notes of distances, integrated with India
information and trappers' accounts, he produced a huge map that is a monument to h

industry and ability as a cartographer. This detail covers the first part of their return journey, from the mouth of the Columbia (left) past the great Cascade peaks to the Rocky Mountain wilderness. At the lower right-hand corner are the Three Forks of the Missouri.

Clark had spent the winter at Fort Clatsop in making a detailed map of their route, which made it clear that it would be very much shorter to cut directly east across the open end of the U.

The captains decided that Lewis, with nine men, would try the short cut and use his extra time to explore the Marias River area. Clark would lead the rest of the party, more or less over their original route, as far as the forks of the Jefferson. Once they had recovered the canoes and cached goods there, Clark's entire group would travel down the Jefferson to the Three Forks. Then Sergeant Ordway would take a canoe party down the Missouri, pick up the baggage at the Great Falls, and meet Lewis at the Marias. Meanwhile Clark and the remainder of the men would cross due east to the still-unexplored Yellowstone River, make canoes, and follow the river to its joining with the Missouri.

It was dangerous to weaken themselves by dividing into three small bands just when they were entering country where they were likely to meet hostile Indians, but the two captains felt it their duty to explore as much of the area as they could before their return to civilization.

On July 3 the two groups separated. As Clark and his men began following the Bitterroot to the south, Lewis' party set off north and then east along the river he had named after his "worthy friend and companion Capt. Clark." Lewis and his men moved along without much difficulty, save from the mosquitoes, which tormented them almost constantly. On July 7 they passed through a gap—now called Lewis and Clark Pass, although Clark never saw it—in a low ridge and found that they had crossed the Continental Divide.

Soon they were among herds of bellowing buffalo, and the hungry days were definitely past. They struck the Medicine River (today called the Sun River) on July 8 and followed it to its mouth just above the Great Falls. By July 13 they were at the spot where they had camped more than a year before.

On opening their cache, they found that high water had flooded it. All the plant specimens Lewis had collected and dried with such care were lost, most of the medicines were ruined, and Lewis' bearskins were spoiled. But a very important chart of the Missouri was safe, and many other articles, though damp, could be dried out.

The mosquitoes were so numerous that the men often inhaled them into their throats; even the dog, Scannon, howled with the torment. Ten of their best horses were stolen by Indians, and Drewyer was absent for three days, tracking them without success. The evening of Drewyer's return, McNeal, another of the party, was surprised by a grizzly and escaped with his life only by climbing a tree. "There seems to be a sertain fatality attatched to . . . these falls," wrote Lewis, under his ragged mosquito net.

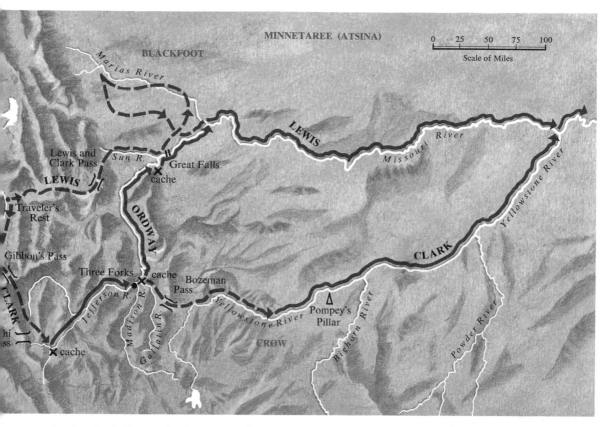

MINNETAREE (ATSINA)

BLACKFOOT

Marias River

LEWIS

Missouri River

Lewis and Clark Pass

Sun R. Great Falls
LEWIS ✕ cache

ORDWAY

Traveler's Rest

CLARK

Yellowstone River

Gibbon's Pass

Three Forks ✕ cache Bozeman Pass

CLARK

hi ss

Jefferson R. *Madison R.* *Gallatin R.* Yellowstone River

Pompey's Pillar

✕ cache

CROW

Bighorn River *Powder River*

0   25   50   75   100
Scale of Miles

*At Traveler's Rest (left) the party split up—
Lewis to explore the Marias River by land,
Clark to retrace their outward route as far
as Three Forks, traveling both overland
(broken line) and by canoe (solid). From
there Ordway went down the Missouri to
rejoin Lewis, while Clark reconnoitered the
Yellowstone and met them below its mouth.*

On July 17 Lewis instructed Sergeant Gass and five men to wait for Ordway's canoe party in order to help in the portaging around the Great Falls. Taking Drewyer and the Fields brothers, the captain headed for the upper waters of the Marias River.

The previous summer everyone but Lewis and Clark had been convinced that the Marias was the true Missouri and led directly into the mountains. Having proved them wrong, the captain now intended to see if any branch of the Marias extended as far north as 50 degrees latitude. If this were so, the river would come close enough to the Saskatchewan River in Canada for a portage to connect the streams, making them into a route for transporting Canadian furs south to American ports.

They struck the Marias and rode toward its headwaters. By July 22 it was clear that no part of the river would reach as far north as 50 degrees latitude. After a wet and hungry exploration, they started back on July 26. There had been many signs of Indian hunting parties, which they knew must have been made either by the warlike Blackfeet or by the tribe they called Minnetarees of Fort de Prairie (actually they were the Atsinas and were not related in any way to the Hidatsa Minnetarees they had made friends with near Fort Mandan).

They were barely eighteen miles on their way to the Missouri, and Drewyer was out ahead when Lewis suddenly sighted a band of eight Indians with about thirty horses.

This was a very unpleasant sight, however I resolved to make the best of our situation and to approach them in a friendly manner. I directed J. Fields to display the flag which I had brought for that purpose and advanced slowly to-

At the confluence of the Marias River (above, left) with the Missouri, Lewis arranged to meet Ordway's canoe party and retrieve the cached goods deposited on the outward journey.

MAXIMILIAN, *Travels in the Interior* . . . , 1834: YALE UNIVERSITY LIBRARY

Thirty years after Lewis' encounter with hostile Indians on the Marias, Bodmer met a party of Blackfeet at a trading fort close to the Great Falls and painted a couple of the proud warriors. Their aristocratic manner impressed even his patron, a German prince.

ward them. About this time they discovered us and appeared to run about in a very confused manner as if much allarmed, their attention had been previously so fixed on Drewyer that they did not discover us untill we had began to advance upon them.

Lewis managed to dispel their confusion and distrust by shaking hands all around and smoking a peace pipe with them. By signs, Lewis gathered that these were Minnetarees of Fort de Prairie, although, in fact, they were Blackfeet. He offered gifts to three chiefs among them, and the Indians accepted his suggestion that they camp together by the river. That evening Drewyer interpreted a speech by Lewis asking them to make peace with their neighbors and inviting them to visit the trading posts that would soon be set up at the mouth of the Marias River.

Although the Indians seemed friendly, Lewis did not trust them. He sat up late smoking with them and kept the first watch himself until the Indians had fallen asleep. Then, turning the watch over to Reuben Fields, Lewis "feel into a profound sleep."

He was awakened at daybreak by a shout from Drewyer: "Damn you, let go my gun!" and Lewis jumped up to discover a dangerous scuffle going on. Joseph Fields, then on watch, had carelessly laid his rifle down beside his sleeping brother, and one of the Indians snatched both guns and ran. Two other warriors instantly pounced upon the guns of Lewis and Drewyer. Joseph woke his brother with a shout; the two ran after the fleeing thief and caught him, and in the struggle Reuben stabbed the Indian through the heart. As for Drewyer, he was wide awake the moment his rifle was

125

In this dramatic version of Lewis' encounter with Black-feet from Gass' Journal, *the captain, in a cocked hat, shoots an Indian who is stealing his horse. The man in a fur cap may be intended for Drewyer, one of Lewis' three (not five) companions, who in 1810 was killed near the Three Forks—by Blackfeet.*

touched and grabbed it back, just as Lewis, reaching for his gun, saw an Indian making off with it. Drawing his pistol, the captain "bid him lay down my gun which he was in the act of doing when the Fieldses returned and drew up their guns to shoot him which I forbid as he did not appear to be about to make any resistance."

The Indians now began driving off all the horses, with the explorers in hot pursuit. Panting for breath, Lewis called out that he would shoot if they did not give him his horse back. In an exchange of shots, a second Indian fell dead. The rest fled, leaving half their horses and nearly all their weapons behind. Lewis picked out four of the best Indian horses to replace his own lost mount and bring his party's total to seven, and while the men saddled up, the captain burned the Indians' bows and arrows and shields on the campfire. This was the first and only time that members of the expedition killed Indians, and Lewis was convinced that the survivors would bring

a large Indian band on their heels, bent on revenge. Since the Indians knew that he intended to meet the rest of his party at the junction of the Marias River and the Missouri, Lewis began to fear that the hostile natives might massacre the other members of the expedition before he could get there to warn them.

Taking some of the Indians' buffalo meat, the four began pushing their horses "as hard as they would bear" toward the Missouri. By dark they were eighty miles from the scene of the attack, but after taking a brief rest, they traveled on again by moonlight and covered another twenty miles before they lay down to sleep at about two in the morning. Their marathon ride had made them all so saddle-sore that they could hardly stand the next day, but Lewis insisted they had not a moment to lose and urged them forward.

As they neared the Missouri, they heard the sound of gunfire "very distinctly on the river to our right," and on arriving at the river bank, "had the unspeakable satisfaction to see our canoes coming down." Sergeant Ordway's ten-man party had made the journey down the Missouri without incident and had been joined at the Great Falls by the six men Lewis had left there. With horses to do the heavy hauling, the sixteen men had portaged canoes and luggage around the Great Falls much more easily than the entire expedition had done on the way upstream. Once the portage was over, Ordway and most of his men took the white pirogue and five canoes downstream, while Gass and Willard set out overland with the horses. As luck would have it, they arrived at the rendezvous only a few hours after the canoe party encountered Lewis.

The caches at the mouth of the Marias River were opened and found in fair condition, although the red pirogue had decayed too much to be worth repair. Freeing the horses, Lewis and his men set out down the Missouri in the rain, eager to leave the danger behind and rejoin their comrades at the mouth of the Yellowstone.

On August 7 they arrived at the Yellowstone River, where Lewis was expecting to meet Clark's party. But the only sign of his fellow captain was a torn note saying that Clark had moved down-river because hunting was poor and the mosquitoes were bad.

Four days later, still behind Clark, they stopped for food, and Lewis and Cruzatte went ashore to shoot elk. Lewis killed one of the animals and Cruzatte wounded another.

We reloaded our guns and took different routs through the thick willows in pursuit of the Elk; I was in the act of firing on the Elk a second time when a ball struck my left thye about an inch below my hip joint, missing the bone it passed through the left thye and cut the thickness of the bullet across the hinder part of the right thye; the stroke was very severe.

"Damn you, you have shot me," Lewis cried out, guessing that Cruzatte had mistaken him for an elk in the dense brush, since the captain wore

Thrown from his horse when a grizzly reared up unexpectedly from the bushes, Hugh McNeal clubbed the bear with his gun and shinnied up a tree. In an engraving from Gass' Journal, he is perched there, minus his musket, while an animal more like Lewis' dog, Scannon, than a grizzly eyes him from below.

127

elk skins and the waterman was blind in one eye and nearsighted in the remaining one. But when there was no answer to his call, the alarming thought occurred that an Indian had shot him. Shouting to Cruzatte to go back to the boats, Lewis at once retreated as fast as his painful wound would permit, calling to the men to arm themselves. The pain grew so intense that he could not lead the men back to rescue Cruzatte. Directing them to go on, he stumbled back to the boats, and with his pistol, rifle, and air gun, prepared "to sell my life as deerly as possible."

The party's dugout canoes were roughly hewn tree trunks like this one, preserved by Idaho Indians because of a tradition that it was built and used by Lewis and Clark.

It did not come to that extremity. In about twenty minutes the men returned with Cruzatte. They had seen no sign of Indians. And although the waterman denied having heard Lewis call to him, it was plain to all that he had shot his captain by mistake and was so embarrassed that he did not want to admit to it.

Being shot in the seat of the pants is not as funny as it may sound. Fortunately the bullet missed bone and artery, but Lewis was in excruciating pain. In a high fever after dressing his own wound with Gass' help, he had to spend the night lying in the pirogue because he could not bear the agony of moving.

The following day they met two fur traders from Illinois who told them that Clark had passed by only the day before. Lewis and his men hurried on in eager expectation.

Now to go back and follow Captain Clark. After the two parties separated at Traveler's Rest on July 3, Clark and twenty men, Sacagawea, the baby, and fifty horses started up the Bitterroot River. But instead of taking the route of the previous year across Lemhi Pass, they found an easier and more direct trail somewhat to the north and crossed the Continental Divide at what was later named Gibbon's Pass.

On July 8 they reached the forks of the Jefferson, where they had sunk their canoes and cached supplies the previous August. The cache contained a quantity of tobacco, and the men,

A "U.S. Capt. M. Lewis" branding iron was found in 1892 on an island in the Columbia.

who had been without any for at least six months, "become so impatient to be chewing it that they scercely gave themselves time to take their saddles off . . . before they were off to the deposit." The precious tobacco and the rest of the cached goods were safe, and although one canoe had a hole in it, it was reparable.

Two days were spent in getting the canoes ready, but once they were afloat, the trip down-river with the swift current was a fast one. In only three days they were at the Three Forks. There the party divided again. Sergeant Ordway and nine men paddled five canoes and most of the baggage down-river to the Great Falls to meet Lewis' men and carry out the portage around the rapids. Meanwhile Clark, with ten men, Sacagawea, and the baby, set out by land toward the Yellowstone River.

This was familiar country to Sacagawea. The Shoshonis regularly hunted in the area, and she had been there many times when she was a child. Without hesitation she directed Clark along a fork of the Gallatin River, then over a pass—later named Bozeman Pass—in a dividing ridge. On the other side they began following a small stream downhill, and barely ten miles farther on, the stream joined the Yellowstone River, already deep and broad at that point.

The only hardship on the fifty-mile journey was suffered by their horses, whose hoofs were worn to the quick by the stony ground. The ingenious Clark solved this by having "Mockersons made of green [untanned] Buffalow Skin and put on their feet which seams to releve them very much."

They followed the river downstream for four days, seeking timber large enough to make dugout canoes. The Yellowstone country, like that of the Missouri, was timbered mainly along the riverbanks. The two largest cottonwoods they could find would make canoes about twenty-eight feet long and barely two feet wide—a tight squeeze for Clark's party and its baggage, even if one of them was a baby. Clark had no other choice but to use these two trees and hope to give his dugouts extra strength by lashing them together. Work began on July 20, and that night roving Indians stole twenty-four of their fifty horses.

By July 23 the canoes were completed, and next morning most of the party embarked, while Sergeant Pryor, with Shannon and Windsor, took the remaining horses overland. Clark had

The captains' joyous report of huge quantities of beaver in the Upper Missouri valleys led countless fur trappers to follow in their footsteps. They brought back such numbers of pelts that ten years after Bodmer saw these beaver on his 1833 trip, the breed was nearly extinct.

instructed Pryor to deliver the horses to the Mandan villages. There he was to barter them for trading goods to be used in negotiations that might persuade the Sioux chiefs to visit Washington—the captains were still hoping to end the Sioux nation's threat to existing and potential river traffic on the Missouri.

With the current behind it, the clumsy double canoe covered the miles swiftly, and before evening the party overtook Pryor. The sergeant was having his troubles. Whenever they came near a herd of buffalo, the horses, trained by the Indians to hunt, would break loose and surround the animals almost as well as if they had riders directing them. Pryor needed an extra man to ride ahead and scare away the buffalo before the horses came up. Hugh Hall, who could not swim, volunteered for the job, and the two groups went their separate ways.

On July 25 Clark's canoe party stopped to examine a landmark visible for miles around—a rock tower, two hundred feet high, rising sheer above the flat plains. Clark, who enjoyed leaving his name on trees as a record of his visit, seized the opportunity to carve "Wm. Clark July 25 1806" on the rock face, already decorated with Indian drawings. He christened the tower after Sacagawea's baby, whom he affectionately called "Pomp"—a Shoshoni word meaning "first-born." To this day it is known as Pompey's Pillar, and Clark's signature can still be seen.

Two days later the Rocky Mountains, which had been continuously in view since May 1, finally vanished in the distance behind them. Clark began noting the tremendous numbers of buffalo, which were then in their mating season and bellowed incessantly. Elk herds rested near the river, too tame to be alarmed as the double canoe passed by, barely twenty paces away. And there were great quantities of beaver, which would soon bring many trappers—including several of the expedition's own men—to these streams in search of pelts.

By the time they reached the junction of the Yellowstone and the Missouri on August 3, the mosquitoes were so thick that the men could neither hunt nor work, and at night, with only their worn blankets for protection, they could scarcely endure the pain. Next afternoon, after leaving a note for Lewis, they went downriver a few miles to camp on a sand bar. Even here there was no relief. The baby's face was puffed and swollen from the stings, and sleep was almost impossible. They continued slowly down the river, blessing every gust of wind that sprang up and kept the mosquitoes off.

On August 8 they were greatly surprised to see Sergeant Pryor and his three men floating down the river toward them in two bullboats—round, basin-shaped craft like those used by the Mandans. They brought the sad news that the Indians had stolen the rest of the horses. Left afoot on the plains, the men had hiked to the river at Pompey's Pillar and made their odd craft by killing a couple of buffalo and stretching their hides over frameworks of saplings.

Three days later the party met Joseph Dickson and Forest Hancock, the two fur trappers whom Lewis would see the following day. From them they learned that the peace the captains had arranged between the Mandans and Hidatsa Minnetarees on the one hand and the Arikaras on the other had not lasted long, for the two sides were at war once more.

At 1 P.M. on August 12 Clark's party was overtaken by Lewis' boats. Their first joy turned to alarm when they failed to see Lewis with the party. Clark soon discovered him lying in the pirogue and was able to dress his wound and confirm that, though extremely painful, it was not dangerous.

OVERLEAF: *Curving through what is now the fertile farmland of the Paradise Valley in southern Montana, the Yellowstone River runs past the Absaroka Mountains. Thanks to Sacagawea's guidance, Clark reached the Yellowstone with ease over Bozeman Pass.*
RAY ATKESON

Lewis, who had kept up his journal while immobilized, made one last entry and then thankfully abandoned his duties to Clark. While they were camping and exchanging some of their news, Dickson and Hancock caught up with them; the trappers wanted to revisit the Mandans.

It took the party only two more days to reach the Minnetaree and Mandan villages, where they received a joyful reception. But the Indians resisted Clark's attempt to persuade some of the chiefs to accompany the party to Washington; the Indians insisted that they would never pass alive through the country of the Sioux down-river. At last, however, Clark had some success: a Mandan chief named Sheheke, or Big White, agreed to make the trip.

Clark solemnly scolded the chiefs for breaking the peace with the Arikaras. The abashed Minnetarees and Mandans gave excuses, but they agreed to try again and asked him to tell the Arikaras that they could come and visit without fear.

Private John Colter now came to the captains with a request to be discharged from the service. Dickson and Hancock had invited him to join their trapping venture up the Missouri in the country from which he had just come. Colter, who had seen the big sky and the wide land, had no desire to return to civilization even for a brief fling. The captains agreed to discharge him, provided that no one else wanted the same privilege. No one

else did. "We gave Jo Colter Some Small articles which we did not want and some powder & lead. the party also gave him several articles which will be usefull to him on his expedition," wrote Clark.

Charbonneau was also paid off, since there would be no further interpreting duties for him or for Sacagawea. Clark, who had grown very fond of little Pomp, offered to take Charbonneau's son,

a butifull promising child who is 19 months old to which they both himself & wife wer willing provided the child had been weened. they observed that in one year the boy would be sufficiently old to leave his mother & he would then take him to me if I would be so freindly as to raise the child for him in such a manner as I thought proper, to which I agreed &c.

By the last Mails:

MARYLAND. BALTIMORE, OCT. 29, 1806.

A LETTER from *St. Louis (Upper Louisiana),* dated *Sept.* 23, 1806; announces the arrival of Captains LEWIS and CLARK, from their expedition into the interior.—They went to the *Pacific Ocean;* have brought some of the natives and curiosities of the countries through which they passed, and only lost one man. They left the *Pacific Ocean* 23d March, 1806, where they arrived in November, 1805;—and where some American vessels had been just before.—They state the Indians to be as numerous on the *Columbia* river, which empties into the *Pacific,* as the whites in any part of the U. S. They brought a family of the Mandan indians with them. The winter was very mild on the *Pacific.*—They have kept an ample journal of their tour; which will be published; and must afford much intelligence.

On November 5, 1806, the Columbian Centinel *of Boston, Massachusetts, carried a short notice "By the last Mails" on a back page. Its news would have stopped the presses today: the Corps of Discovery was home!*

On August 17 they started on their way again, and four days later, arrived at the first Arikara village. After renewing friendships, Clark brought up the matter of the broken peace agreement, and the Arikaras smoked with Big White, the Mandan chief, and agreed to be at peace again.

As August drew to an end, Clark happily noted that "my worthy friend Capt. Lewis is recovering fast," although he later taxed his strength by trying to walk too soon and had a brief relapse. On August 30 a number of Teton Sioux hailed them from shore, but Clark lectured them, through an interpreter, on their bad conduct of two years before and refused to have anything further to do with them. On September 4 they stopped to visit Sergeant Floyd's grave and found it had been opened by Indians who had buried a chief's son to share Floyd's journey to another world. Distressed, they reburied their comrade more securely.

There were numerous trappers and traders going upstream from whom they were able to buy much-needed provisions and cut down the time spent in hunting. Indeed, some of the traders, considering them as men returned from the grave, pressed on them gifts of food and whiskey—the first they had tasted since a celebration held on July 4, 1805. As they hastened downstream, with the current behind them, Clark noted their mileage in his journal, and the word "only" began to appear even before

figures of more than sixty or seventy miles a day.

On September 20 some of the party raised a happy shout at seeing cows on the bank. Shortly afterward, they came in sight of La Charrette, the last civilized settlement they had seen on their way upriver and now the first one on their return. They stopped overnight as the guests of two young traders whose boat was tied up at the bank and were told by the delighted villagers that they had long since been given up as lost.

The next day they reached St. Charles, and "the party rejoiced at the Sight . . . plyed thear ores with great dexterity." Saluting their friends with three rounds from their blunder-busses, the men landed and were met by excited townspeople. After the Mandan chief Sheheke had been outfitted with some clothes from "the publick store," their boats left the Missouri and were swept down the Mississippi the short distance to St. Louis. On September 23, 1806, the whole town turned out to welcome the "Robinson Crusoes—dressed entirely in buckskins," as one newspaper account described them.

Two years four months after it had begun, the long journey was over. Captain Lewis at once wrote a note to detain the United States mails at Cahokia for his first thrilling dispatch to President Jefferson, and three days later Clark made the final entry in the lengthy journals: "a fine morning. we commenced wrighting &c."

THE WONDERS MISSED

If Clark had turned upstream instead of down when he reached the Yellowstone River in July, 1806, he would have entered a region so extraordinary that his reports of it probably would have been disbelieved. As it was, the first white man to glimpse the wonders of the Yellowstone area was John Colter, who left the returning party to go fur trapping in the wilderness. In 1807 Colter set off alone from a trading fort on the Bighorn River on a journey that took him as far as the Grand Tetons. In its course he discovered at least some of the spouting and steaming geyser basins around Yellowstone Lake,

perhaps even marveled at the river thundering through the rainbow-colored chasm of the Yellowstone's Grand Canyon. But Colter, an uneducated man, never wrote down his experiences. After his death in 1813, stories of "Colter's Hell" became half-believed rumors, recirculated from time to time as fur trappers penetrated the area during the 1830's. Serious exploration began three decades later, and in 1870 a party led by General Henry Washburn spent a month there, bringing back such historic records as a private's sketch of cascading Tower Falls (above, right). The next year Fer-

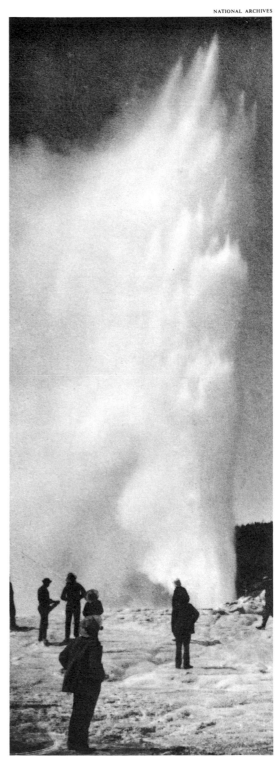

dinand V. Hayden conducted an official government survey of Yellowstone. With him was artist Thomas Moran, who made color sketches of such marvels as the bubbling hot springs on the Gardiner River (above, left). Another member of the group was William H. Jackson, the great photographer of the West. His prints, made from glass-plate negatives, played a vital part in persuading Congress to make Yellowstone into America's first and most famous national park. At right is his view of an astonishing event that has since been recorded by millions of cameras—Old Faithful erupting on cue.

7

THE END OF THE TRAIL

The accomplishments of the expedition had been magnificent in every way. Simply in terms of distance traveled, they were astonishing, for the captains' most careful calculations showed that—fighting river currents, finding trails over towering mountains, meeting and impressing tribe after tribe of Indians—they had covered 4,134 miles from the mouth of the Missouri to the Pacific and 3,555 miles back again.

At St. Louis the tough, disciplined group of young men who made this achievement possible was broken up for good. Once Lewis had paid off his men, he and Clark journeyed together as far as Louisville, Kentucky. Clark stopped off to visit his relatives, while Lewis continued his triumphant journey east, arriving in Washington just after Christmas.

On January 10, 1807, Lewis attended a gala reception at the White House for the "King and Queen of the Mandans"—that is, Sheheke and his wife. Four days later Lewis was the guest of honor at a Washington banquet. Clark, who was to have shared in the honors, was then in Virginia,

wooing a young lady named Julia Hancock, who had been in his thoughts throughout the expedition.

As well as voting double pay for each member of the party, Congress proposed to give 320 acres of land to each enlisted man, 1,000 acres to Clark, and 1,600 to Lewis. However, Lewis refused the offer. He had promised William Clark before they left that their rewards would be equal, and at his urging Congress awarded each captain 1,600 acres.

That same year Lewis was appointed Governor of Louisiana Territory, the northern portion of the Louisiana Purchase, with headquarters in St. Louis. Clark, who had already had the pleasure of returning to the War Department the lieutenant's commission that had so insulted him, was recommissioned as brigadier general of the Louisiana militia.

"Never did a similar event excite more joy thro' the United States," wrote Jefferson of the explorers' return. The hero of the hour, Lewis posed in 1807 wearing buckskins and a magnificent ermine-tailed cape, probably the one presented to him by Cameahwait.

Visiting Washington in 1807, Sheheke, the Mandan chief, was portrayed by Charles de Saint-Mémin. This French artist also did the crayon portrait of Lewis on page 139.

Lewis had been an excellent explorer and soldier, but the problems of politics and administration were foreign to him. As Louisiana passed from the jurisdiction of one country to that of another, land titles had become hopelessly confused. Fur trappers and traders were now plying the Missouri in increasing numbers, and there was trouble with the Indians, who resented the white man's intrusion on their lands.

Life was moving much more smoothly for General Clark. He married Julia Hancock in January, 1808, and brought her to St. Louis that spring to a house that Lewis found for him. Then he began organizing his frontier militia, building a fort on the Missouri, and strengthening the military posts that already existed.

Governor Lewis' problems multiplied. In July, 1809, he received word from Washington that the government would not be responsible for certain expenses he had charged to official business—for instance, five hundred dollars to buy tobacco and powder for the group that had escorted Chief Sheheke back to the Mandans. Already depressed by political difficulties, Lewis now saw himself on the brink of financial ruin.

Selling some of his land grants to clear up debts, he collected the receipts for the disputed items and set out for Washington to explain his problems in person. He started down the Mississippi on September 4, 1809, planning to take ship from New Orleans to the capital. Halfway there, he changed his mind and decided to go overland instead. When he left the boat at Chickasaw Bluffs (Memphis), he was ill and behaving very oddly.

He wrote to President Madison—a letter filled with crossed-out words, in a scrawl quite unlike his usual neat handwriting. He visited the Army post, Fort Pickering, where his strange behavior so alarmed old Army friends that they concluded he was mentally disturbed. On September 30 his little party left Chickasaw Bluffs and headed east for one of the famous trails of America: the Natchez Trace.

The Trace, a series of old Indian trails, ran from Natchez, Mississippi, to Nashville, Tennessee. Since most of its travelers were boatmen returning north with their profits from taking cargoes down-river to New Orleans, it was infested with robbers and cutthroats. On October 10 Lewis' party stopped for the night at a place called Grinder's Stand in Tennessee. It was nothing more than two cabins and a stable in a small clearing, owned by a Robert Grinder, who provided travelers with meals, liquor, and beds.

When everyone had gone to bed, a shot was heard, then a second, from the cabin where Lewis was sleeping by himself (his two servants had been put up in the stable). Mrs. Grinder, fearful because her husband was away, peered through the chinks in her cabin wall and in the dim light saw Lewis stagger out of his cabin and over to her door, crying out for water and entreating her to take care of his wounds. Hour after hour, he kept begging for help, but Mrs. Grinder kept the door firmly closed. Not until dawn did she send her children to the stable to rouse Lewis' two servants, who, strangely enough, had heard nothing.

They found that Lewis, terribly wounded in the side and the head, had managed to crawl back to his cabin. He begged his servants to end his agonies by killing him with his own gun. Later that morning his body was found sprawled beside the road.

Lewis' mysterious and tragic death, at the age of thirty-five, seemed to be a suicide. Mrs. Grinder gave evidence that he had been acting strangely the evening before he died. Even Thomas Jefferson was convinced that his friend had killed himself. But the man who found his body believed that Lewis had been shot in the back, possibly by robbers. There were no powder burns on his clothing or flesh, as there would have been if he had shot himself. His pocketbook was gone and his trunks of papers were in total confusion.

The dead governor's financial affairs were almost hopelessly snarled. General Clark, his executor, did what he could to straighten things out, but it took six years for the lawyer handling the estate to make his final report. All Lewis' remaining money, land, and other property had not been enough to pay his debts.

The two captains had hoped that publication of their journals and the detailed information they had taken such pains to record would bring them fortune as well as fame. After Lewis' death, with not a line of the manuscript written, Clark took over the task of arranging to publish their joint work. In 1810 he persuaded Nicholas Biddle, later president of the Bank of the United States, to edit the immense mass of material into publishable shape. Although Biddle did a superb job—for which he would accept neither pay nor credit—there was endless trouble in getting the two-volume edition of the "History of the Expedition Under the Command of Captains Lewis and Clark" into print. Two years after its publication in 1814 Clark still had not been sent a copy.

In 1813 Clark was appointed Governor of Missouri Territory, which was actually Lewis' old post, renamed.

RELICS OF THE PAST

The specimens and artifacts sent by the captains from Fort Mandan in the spring of 1805 filled four boxes, three cages, and a large trunk. In the returning expedition's baggage the following year were furs, seeds, horns, Indian handicrafts—Mandan pottery, conical sea-grass hats made by the Clatsops, and Sioux tobacco pouches decorated with porcupine quills and tin—and such mementos as the amulets, or protective charms, taken by Lewis from the shields of the slain Blackfeet on the Marias River. Many of these were exhibited in Charles Willson Peale's museum in Philadelphia. When this was split up, a few precious items were preserved at Harvard University. One of these is a Cree woman's dress (right), the oldest existing example of Plains Indian beadwork. The Columbia big-leaf maple (left) was one of the botanical specimens taken to England for cataloguing by Frederick Pursh but eventually sent back to Philadelphia. Some trophies, like the horn from a Rocky Mountain bighorn (far left), were proudly handed down in the captains' families. The most evocative relic is the elk-skin-bound diary (top, left) that Clark carried on his knee to record rough field notes for later transcription in his journal.

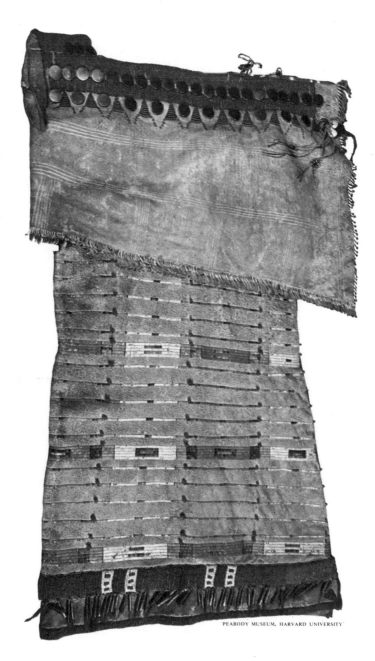

PEABODY MUSEUM, HARVARD UNIVERSITY

143

He was also made Superintendent of Indian Affairs. Since the War of 1812 was in progress, Clark spent two years checking British efforts to arouse the Indians. One measure of his success is that, although Indian raids took place, there was no outright war.

Unlike his friend Lewis, Clark was an extremely successful territorial governor, although he did not much enjoy the position. Thanks to his ability to get things done without fuss, he managed to spend seven years in office without making a single enemy. When Missouri became a state in 1821, he was forced against his will to run for governor and was probably quite relieved when he was defeated.

His work as Superintendent of Indian Affairs continued, however, although his responsibility was now limited to those tribes north and west of the new state. He held this position until his death, seventeen years later. Clark's understanding and respect for Indian ways and viewpoints played a vital part in opening up the vast lands that his expedition had first traversed. In return, the Indians honored and trusted him, and those who came to St. Louis were always welcomed at the home of their "Red Head Chief."

Among Clark's many visitors were Charbonneau and Sacagawea, who brought their son Baptiste for Clark to raise, as he had promised, "as my own child." Charbonneau tried farming but soon tired of it and went back up the Missouri in 1811. Baptiste and his little sister stayed behind, with Clark as their guardian, and when the boy was about nineteen, he was befriended by a visiting German prince, who took him to Europe for five years. After his return Baptiste guided many travelers into the western wilderness, and he ended his days among the Shoshoni Indians in the Rockies.

So, probably, did his mother, although there are conflicting stories and it is difficult to be sure. In later years, an old woman named Sacagawea lived among the Shoshonis. She knew many small details of the Lewis and Clark expedition, and Baptiste acknowledged her as his mother. When she died in 1884, the papers that would have proved her story unfortunately were buried with her. Her grave can still be seen on the Wind River Indian Reservation in Wyoming.

There are conflicting stories also about Clark's servant York, who had so much impressed every Indian on their route. In time Clark freed him and set him up in the freight-hauling business with a wagon and six horses. But York had bad luck. Two of his horses died; he sold the others and went to work for wages. Clark believed that he had died of cholera in Tennessee while on his way to enter his old master's service once more.

However, living among the Crow Indians in 1832 was a Negro who claimed to have come to the country first with Lewis and Clark. He was a chief, with four wives, who was treated by the Indians with much respect. It would be pleasant to believe that this

Clark named Montana's Judith River after a lady he mistakenly called Judy. Julia Hancock's portrait explains why Clark remembered her face, if not her name. Later, as his wife, she ran his rambling country home near St. Louis (left), where Indians were constant visitors.

was how York really ended his days.

Clark tried to keep in touch with members of the expedition when he could. A list of names with his annotations shows that several men were killed fighting Indians, among them Cruzatte and Drewyer.

But most of the men who had gone with the captains vanished into obscurity once again. They probably returned to their farms, or more likely, settled on the frontier. Just as Thomas Jefferson had foreseen, the land they had discovered was filling up fast with new settlers. At first they clung to the banks of the Missouri; then their homesteads began rising on the fertile plains beyond. The Upper Missouri attracted thousands of fur trappers and buffalo hunters, who risked scalp-ing to make fortunes from beaver pelts and buffalo robes.

The Indians were becoming openly hostile, resentful of the white men and ruined by their whiskey. In 1830 Clark, who had noted in 1804 how the Arikaras refused to drink liquor at all, wrote sadly: "Not an Indian could be found among a thousand who would not . . . sell his horse, his gun, or his last blanket, for another drink."

In 1811 John Jacob Astor sent his agents to the Pacific over the route the captains had pioneered. America's first million-dollar fortune was to be built upon profits from Astoria, the fur-trading post they set up at the mouth of the Columbia.

Later, as the wagon trains began to roll down the Oregon Trail, farms sprang up farther inland along the Willamette River, which Clark had discovered.

By 1870, when Patrick Gass, the expedition's last white survivor, died at the ripe age of ninety-nine, the continental limits of the United States stood where they are today. Just the year before, a railroad to California had been completed. The journey from the Mississippi to the Pacific that had taken the expedition eighteen months of toil could now be made in comparative ease in a week or less—but over a different course.

Lewis and Clark were convinced that their trail up the Missouri and over the Rockies would become a

Far to the south of Lewis and Clark's first crossing of the Divide, a later wagon train fords a creek near Fort Laramie, carrying hopeful settlers westward on the Oregon Trail.

valuable trading route, but later explorers discovered far easier ways of reaching the Pacific. The Oregon Trail cut directly across the plains and the mountains—from Independence, Missouri, to Fort Vancouver, Washington. The Mormons with their handcarts, the gold rushers, the emigrants to California, all used the Trail and

still other routes farther to the south.

In other ways, too, the expedition fell short of original expectations. None of the men made his fortune out of joining the party. Jefferson's hopes of publishing the captains' detailed notes on natural history and geography were not fulfilled until they had lost much of their scientific value. A distinguished mathematician, after struggling to make sense of the celestial observations on which Lewis had spent so much time, abandoned the project in despair.

Nonetheless, the expedition's contribution remains an extraordinary one. It brought back definite information about an area that had hitherto been a void to Americans and specimens of animals and plants that were unknown to science. The captains' survey work helped establish America's claim to the Oregon country, and Clark's maps were the first reasonably accurate delineation of land that was to add ten more states to the Union.

Most important, Lewis and Clark's achievements inspired other men to follow them and to enlarge their discoveries. Covering the explorers' route today, past thriving cities, massive dams and vast reservoirs, patterned fields of grain extending to the horizon, it is hard to visualize the wilderness that these men first charted. Yet, no matter how much the landscape they knew has been changed or how swiftly and easily the journey can be made, nothing can alter this truth: Lewis and Clark showed the way.

THOMAS JEFFERSON,

PRESIDENT

OF THE UNITED STATES OF AMERICA.

From the powers vested in us and —— by the above authority : To all who shall see these presents, Greeting:

KNOW YE, that from the special confidence reposed by us in the sincere and unalterable attachment of *War charpa the Sticker a Warrior chief* of the *Soeus* NATION to the UNITED STATES; as also from the abundant proofs given by him of his amicable disposition to cultivate peace, harmony, and good neighbourhood with the said States, and the citizens of the same ; we do by the authority vested in us, require and charge, all citizens of the United States, all Indian Nations, in treaty with the same, and all other persons whomsoever, to *receive* acknowledge, and treat the said *War Charpa* the *Sticker* in the most friendly manner, declaring him to be the friend and ally of the said States: the government of which will at all times be extended to *his* protection, so long as *he* do acknowledge the authority of the same.

Having signed with our hands and affixed our seals this *Thirtyfirst* day of *August* 180 *four*

M. Lewis Capt.
1st U.S. Reg. Infy.

W. Clark Capt. &c.

Both captains signed and sealed this "Indian commission," given a Sioux warrior in 1804, Lewis with his regular Army rank, Clark as "Captn on an Expdn. for N.W. Discovery."

AMERICAN HERITAGE JUNIOR LIBRARY

JOSEPH L. GARDNER, *Editor*

Janet Czarnetzki, *Art Director*

Jean Atcheson, *Associate Editor*

Sandra L. Russell, *Copy Editor*

Kathleen Fitzpatrick, *Assistant Copy Editor*

Laurie B. Platt, *Picture Editor*

Cynthia Feldman, *Picture Researcher*

ACKNOWLEDGMENTS

The Editors would like to thank the following individuals and institutions for their generous assistance:

American Philosophical Society, Philadelphia, Pennsylvania—Gertrude Hess

Amon Carter Museum of Western Art, Fort Worth, Texas—Mrs. J. E. Devine

Thomas Jefferson Memorial Foundation, Charlottesville, Virginia—James Bear, Jr.

Joslyn Art Museum, Omaha, Nebraska—Mildred Goosman

The Mutter Museum, College of Physicians of Philadelphia, Pennsylvania—Mrs. Ella Wade

National Archives and Records Service, Washington, D.C.—A. P. Muntz

National Park Service, United States Department of the Interior, Washington, D.C.—Frederick R. Bell

Nez Percé National Historic Park, Spalding, Idaho—Robert L. Burns

Peabody Museum, Harvard University, Cambridge, Massachusetts—Mrs. Katherine B. Edsall

The Beinecke Rare Book and Manuscript Library, Yale University, New Haven, Connecticut—Archibald Hanna

Maps by Francis & Shaw, Inc.

FURTHER REFERENCE

Lewis and Clark transcribed their rough notes of each day's events into twenty small notebooks. As each was filled, it was put into a small tin box and sealed to keep it waterproof. Thanks to these precautions, all their completed journals survived the arduous trip and seventeen are now in the collection of the American Philosophical Society in Philadelphia. The Missouri Historical Society in St. Louis has some more journal material, much of the captains' correspondence, and some interesting portraits and personal possessions. Clark's maps and his rough diaries for the early part of the trip are in the Western Americana collections at the Yale University Library. Harvard's Peabody Museum has some of the captains' Indian specimens, while Lewis' surviving botanical specimens are on view at the Philadelphia Academy of Natural Sciences. The stages of the expedition's journey can be followed by marker systems in each state they visited. The Department of the Interior is considering the establishment of a Lewis and Clark National Wilderness Waterway on the Upper Missouri between Fort Benton and Fort Peck Reservoir in Montana, to preserve one of the most fascinating sections of the river almost as the explorers first saw it.

The following books are recommended for further reading:

Bakeless, John, *Lewis and Clark: Partners in Discovery*. Morrow, 1947.

Coues, Elliott, ed., *History of the Expedition Under the Command of Lewis and Clark*, 4 vols. Harper, 1893. Republished in paperback, 3 vols. Dover, 1965.

De Voto, Bernard, *The Course of Empire*. Houghton Mifflin, 1952.

De Voto, Bernard, ed., *The Journals of Lewis and Clark*. Houghton Mifflin, 1953.

Dillon, Richard, *Meriwether Lewis; A Biography*. Coward-McCann, 1965.

Jackson, Donald, ed., *Letters of the Lewis and Clark Expedition with Related Documents, 1783-1854*. University of Illinois Press, 1962.

Josephy, Alvin M., Jr., ed., *The American Heritage Book of Natural Wonders*. American Heritage, 1963.

Josephy, Alvin M., Jr., ed., *The American Heritage History of the Great West*. American Heritage, 1965.

Ketchum, Richard M., ed., *The American Heritage Book of the Pioneer Spirit*. American Heritage, 1959.

Osgood, Ernest S., ed., *The Field Notes of Captain William Clark, 1803-1805*. Yale University Press, 1964.

Quaife, Milo M., ed., *The Journals of Captain Meriwether Lewis and Sergeant John Ordway*. State Historical Society of Wisconsin, 1965.

Salisbury, Albert and Jane, *Two Captains West*. Superior Publishing Co., Seattle, 1950.

Thwaites, Reuben G., ed., *Original Journals of the Lewis and Clark Expedition*, 8 vols. Dodd, Mead, 1905.

Tomkins, Calvin, *The Lewis and Clark Trail*. Harper, 1965.

Wheeler, Olin D., *The Trail of Lewis and Clark, 1804-1904*, 2 vols. Putnam, 1904.

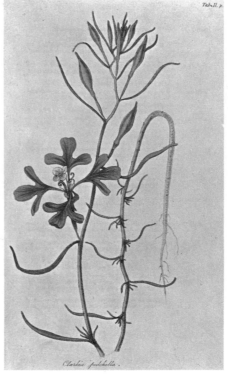

A rose-colored musk (left) and an evening primrose were drawn and classified from Lewis' specimens by German botanist Frederick Pursh, for his authoritative work on American flora. The captains collected so many previously unknown plants that Pursh named two new botanical groupings, or genera, Lewisia *and* Clarkia.

INDEX

Boldface indicates pages on which maps or illustrations appear